PREGNANT TOO SOON

PREGNANT TOO SOON
ADOPTION IS AN OPTION

By Jeanne Warren Lindsay

Illustrated by Pam Patterson Morford

Morning
Glory
Press

Buena Park, California

Library of Congress Cataloging-in-Publication Data

Lindsay, Jeanne Warren
    Pregnant too soon.

    Bibliography: p. 213-218
    Includes index.
    1. Adoption–United States. 2. Pregnancy,
Adolescent–United States. 3. Adolescent mothers–
United States. I. Morford, Pam Patterson. II. Title.
HV875.L48 1988   362.7'34'0973   87-22042
ISBN 0-930934-26-1
ISBN 0-930934-25-3 (pbk.)

MORNING GLORY PRESS, INC.
6595 San Haroldo Way   Buena Park, CA 90620
Telephone (714) 828-1998

To the Courageous Young Women
Who Share Their Lives
on These Pages

CONTENTS

Foreword 11

Preface 15

Acknowledgments 19

1. TO BE OR NOT TO BE –
   A SCHOOL-AGE PARENT 23
   *Parenthood by choice? Possible results of early
   pregnancy; Marriage often no solution; Who is
   my mother?*

2. ARE YOU READY
   FOR PARENTHOOD? 35
   *Questions to ponder; Beth's family today; Beth
   changes schools; Robin decides to parent; Her
   parents' reaction; Erin's life; Consider all
   options; Am I ready to be a parent?*

**3. HOW ADOPTION WORKS –
AGENCIES**   53

*Help from Lisa's counselor; Her friends oppose
adoption; Agency selects adoptive families;
Preparing adoptive parents; "I'm going to be a
doctor"; Baby's father not involved. Jennifer's
dilemma.*

4. MORE ABOUT LEGAL MATTERS   69

*Baby has two birth certificates; Information
requirement act; Jodie's decision; What about
marriage; A memorable Christmas; Ronda –
pregnant again; Adoptive parents pay
counseling fees; Foster care.*

5. INDEPENDENT ADOPTION   83

*Anne meets adoptive parents; Hospital nurse is
supportive; Lawyer's role; Birthparents meet
adoptive parents; Costs of adoption; Experienced lawyer is preferable; Wendi Sue chooses
baby's parents; Lack of counseling may be a
problem.*

6. SOMETIMES RELATIVES ADOPT   99

*Possible problems in relative adoption; Lynn's
story; Lynn decides to enroll in Teen Mother
Program; Lynn's sister will parent; Dear
Abby's advice helps; Vera tries parenting;
Vera makes a decision; Adoptive mother explains; Minority adoption; Special adoption
law for Native Americans; Common criticism
of relative adoption.*

7. FATHERS HAVE RIGHTS 115

*California law; Two "kinds" of fathers; Should
Dennis keep his baby? Mario's decision;
Father can stop adoption; Protecting fathers'
rights.*

8. DEALING WITH GRIEF 125

*Seeing baby before adoption; Hurting doesn't
mean it's wrong decision; Your rights as a
birthparent; Fathers grieve too; Poem by
Gibran may help birthparent.*

9. BIRTHPARENTS WRITE LETTERS 137

*Cyndi shares her feelings; Another birthmother
writes to adoptive parents; Father writes letter;
Leeann's plans change; Key ring is symbol of
baby's love.*

**10. RELEASING TODDLER
FOR ADOPTION** 151

*Who am I? Child's age at relinquishment;
Michele's life changes; Phyllis says she's
mother too soon; Susie and Ed choose a family;
Letitia meets her new family; She'll never
forget Letitia.*

11. ADOPTEES GROW UP 167

*Guess what? I'm adopted! Adoptee searches
for birthparents; Parents find their birthson;
She's curious about birthmother; Many
adoptees never search.*

12. ADOPTIVE PARENTS' EXPERIENCES   181
*Pregnancy impossible for many couples;
Johnson family is described; Hoffmans choose
open adoption; They are chosen – they adopt
Shontel; Only child is adopted.*

**13. MAKING THE DECISION:
WILL I PARENT NOW?**   195

APPENDIX

    Help for Parents   203

    Working with Birthparents   209

    Annotated Bibliography   213

    Index   221

FOREWORD

Every year hundreds of thousands of teenagers are faced with the unexpected news that they are pregnant. From that moment on, lives are changed. There are a whole series of decisions to be made, challenges to be met, and obstacles to be overcome.

The decision of whether or not to parent a child is one of the most difficult anyone could ever be called upon to make. It depends on many factors and impacts the lives of many people. To explore this issue taps the deepest emotions. To be willing to explore the choice of adoption takes tremendous insight and courage.

I have been privileged to work with many young people as they explored their choices. I have been amazed by their willingness to search their hearts and minds for answers. I have been awed by their courage and their love. They must process a tremendous amount of information, sorting myths from facts, contemplating pros and cons, and searching out resources. At times the amount of information that has to be processed seems endless.

At the same time they must continually respond to their hearts. There is a deep bond that grows with the unborn

child that one carries. There is a great longing to do what is
best for that child. An adoption plan is truly born of love
and commitment.

Those of us who work with young people during this
time of decision-making have a tremendous responsibility.
It is up to us to make sure that our assistance is objective
and our information is accurate. It also demands that we
continue to grow ourselves. We have to be willing to offer
the kind of support that is truly helpful. It is never a time
for offering advice.

Ultimately the answers must come from within each
young person. The implications of the choices should not
be viewed lightly. This one decision profoundly and perma-
nently affects the lives of the young birthparents, their
children, their families, and their friends.

Some teenage parents do an excellent job of childrearing.
However, the majority report that they experience far
greater demands than they had anticipated. The adolescent's
own maturational processes may make parenting particu-
larly difficult. Because of their youth, these young people
often face serious financial, educational, social, and emotional challenges.

In *Pregnant Too Soon* Ms. Lindsay helps the reader
realistically evaluate her capabilities to meet the physical
and emotional needs of her child. This is not an easy task,
as one may not fully realize what it means to be a parent
until actually faced with the responsibilities of parenthood.

Pregnant teens often feel that the decision to release a
child is a selfish or uncaring act. Ms. Lindsay presents the
decision to relinquish in a far more positive and realistic
light, showing that it can be a very loving and mature
decision. Her approach is sensitive to the needs of both
mother and child. This quality of sensitivity and insight is
the result of her experience in working intimately with
childbearing adolescents. Her own nurturant and caring
attitude is evident throughout the book.

Pregnant Too Soon: Adoption Is an Option is the most useful book I have found for helping teenagers with this process of decision-making. It provides them with accurate, practical information about adoption. It offers answers to their questions and brings up things they have not contemplated.

This book is also extremely useful in dealing with the emotional side of the decision. It brings the reader closer to others who have faced the same challenges. The case studies, so characteristic of Jeanne Lindsay's work, are valuable in the discovering of one's own feelings. It can be validating to know that others have been through similar situations, felt similar emotions, and struggled with similar decisions.

The author's professional skill is apparent in the thoroughness of her exploration of the topic. The ramifications of adoption, as well as the humanness of the people involved, are well presented.

I recommend that everyone who is closely involved with the adoption option read this book, whether you are an expectant parent, a grandparent, an adoptive parent, a friend, or a professional. It will give you help – objective help – in sorting things out for yourself.

Earlier I said that deciding whether to place one's baby with another family or to rear this child oneself is one of the most difficult decisions anyone will ever be called upon to make. It is also important to emphasize that this can be a positive and growth-producing time. I have watched young people come out of this process much clearer about who they are and what they believe. Most important, I have watched them feel peaceful with having made a conscious decision, one that they believed was right. If you are going through this decision now, I urge you to make the most of it, learn all you can, and trust in yourself.

Those of us who work with pregnant teenagers can be grateful to Ms. Lindsay for filling a long-time gap. This

book was the first comprehensively to present adoption as a
viable option. It brings balance back into the exploration of
alternatives.

I am delighted with this new revised edition of *Pregnant
Too Soon.*

Catherine Monserrat, M.A., Family Therapist
Co-Author, *Teenage Pregnancy: A New Beginning* and
         Working with Childbearing Adolescents

August, 1987

PREFACE

Teenage pregnancy – is it an epidemic? Is it curable?
The answer to both questions is mostly "No." The
percentage of teenagers giving birth has actually declined
during the past 20 years. As for being curable – the teenage
pregnancy phenomenon is far too complex to speak of
simple cures.

While there is no quick fix for the problems surrounding
an unplanned pregnancy, whatever the individual's age,
there are several options. Most young women and their
partners think in terms of three of these options: abortion,
single parenthood or marriage. The fourth option, adoption,
is chosen by less then five percent of all single teenage
mothers in the United States.

The first edition of *Pregnant Too Soon* was published in
1980. Since that time, the percentage of teenage mothers
who aren't married continues to rise, and the adoption rate
has fallen even lower. Teenage parenthood is a fact of life
for many of our young people, and marriage often is not a
good solution.

For most, there is no truly good solution for premature
pregnancy, but there are viable options. Adoption is one of

these options, and I think a trend may be developing toward more interest in adoption among young people. I feel this will happen because of the variety of options now offered within adoption.

Today in many communities, birthparents can be and sometimes are urged to be deeply involved in the adoption plan for their child. No longer are they expected to turn their already-loved baby blindly over to someone they have not selected. As we move toward more open adoption, this option may become a more acceptable alternative to too-early parenthood.

This book, however, is not about "open" adoption. It is, rather, about birthmothers and birthfathers and their decisions. Most of the young people on these pages chose adoption, while a few are rearing their children themselves. They all share their hopes and their dreams, their reasons for choosing (or not choosing) adoption.

I have worked with pregnant teenagers during fifteen years of teaching a self-contained day-long public school class offered as an option to pregnant students. After spending many school days with each of these young women during her pregnancy, a close bond is often created between us.

Because we have an Infant Center on campus which cares for their babies while they attend school, many young mothers choose to stay at our small alternative school after they leave the "pregnant" class. Each student may stay in the special class while she is pregnant and for one semester after her baby is born. Most of these high school mothers continue coming to my room for a daily parenting class while they are attending the high school.

I see many of these young women doing a good job of parenting. I know of no research "proving" that a 16-year-old is necessarily a less able mother than is a woman of 25. The young women I know care a great deal about their babies, give them lots of love, and often cope remarkably well with the responsibilities and extra problems associated with being a very young and, often, a single mother.

After this close association with nearly 1000 pregnant teenagers, however, I am disturbed that the majority do not appear to *choose* motherhood. They simply assume that because they are pregnant and have chosen not to have an abortion, they *must* become mothers.

I can empathize with them – I have five children, and they weren't all "planned" babies. My husband and I never considered making an adoption plan for any of our children. (Except perhaps when we had four teenagers at once for a couple of years!) I don't think it makes a lot of difference in feelings that I was 22 and married when I had my first baby. Being 15 and single doesn't eliminate those feelings of love and caring that most people have for their babies.

Many of the million teenagers who become pregnant each year make a choice. Slightly less than half terminate pregnancy through induced abortion. This is a choice which, I think, must be available to every woman who is pregnant. Every woman should know she has this choice.

However, abortion is seldom mentioned in this book. By the time I meet them, the young women with whom I work have already decided against abortion. Otherwise they would not be enrolling in a class for pregnant students. Their remaining and ever-narrowing choices are marriage (sometimes), single motherhood, and adoption.

If I had written *Pregnant Too Soon* thirty years ago when most pregnant and unmarried teenagers were placing their babies for adoption, this would have been a very different book. I probably would have discussed ways of dealing with, perhaps encouraging, single motherhood, because at that time it wasn't the accepted thing to do.

Today *adoption* is not "the thing to do" according to many people, both adults and teenagers. I'm uncomfortable with both approaches – either expecting almost *all*

teenagers to release or expecting *each one* to keep her
baby. I think the leading lady in this drama, the young
mother, too often has been – and still is – pressured into
making a decision because *other people* think it's right
for her.

But *she* must make this decision herself. Since our culture
today appears to accept single motherhood more easily than
it accepts adoption, much of our literature is devoted to
single parenting. This book is an attempt to even the score a
little – an attempt to show adoption as a viable option to
ill-timed parenthood.

"When I was thinking about adoption, I wished there had
been more to read," a student commented. "You gave me a
few things, but I wanted to know more about how other
people *felt*. I read a lot of books about how the adoption
agencies work, what happens afterward, etc., but there was
nothing that compared the feelings of people who gave
their babies up for adoption and people who kept their
babies. I wanted to compare those feelings."

In this book, young women who released their babies for
adoption and young women who kept their children share
their feelings about and attitudes toward adoption. All the
stories about and quotes from teenagers are real. All the
events described actually happened. Names and minor details have been changed to protect the privacy of the young
people involved. Only exception to these masked identities
is Julie Gomoll whose story appears in Chapter One.

Pregnant Too Soon is certainly not a plea for all pregnant
teenagers – or all those under 18 – or even all those under
15 – to release their babies for adoption. It is, rather, a book
dedicated to the principle that parenthood is such a great
experience for many people that it deserves to be a *chosen*
state of being.

Many pregnant teenagers do not realize that adoption is,
indeed, an option.

ACKNOWLEDGMENTS

Several people were especially helpful as I worked on this revised edition of *Pregnant Too Soon*. Several chapters have been completely rewritten and the others are updated as needed. Some additional accounts of personal experiences are included.

Janice Wills again freely shared the expertise she has gained from years of working with the Los Angeles County Department of Children's Services. Julie Vetica shared ideas gained from her years of working in a pregnant minor program.

Lillian Gonzalez, Director of Adoptions, Christian Counseling and Placement Service, Portales, New Mexico, provided most of the beautiful letters featured in chapter 9.

I am especially grateful to the young women who tell their stories on these pages. They wanted to help. Over and over I heard, "Perhaps my story will help someone else." Working and talking with them has been a privilege.

Several adoptees and adoptive parents share their lives in chapters 11 and 12. They, too, are very special people. Most of them were referred to me by Jennifer Stebbins and

Rachel Bublitz, Christian Adoption and Family Service, Anaheim, California.

Many others discussed adoption with me including attorneys David Leavitt and James Edson.

Jennifer Myers-Rick, an adoptee who has worked with pregnant teenagers, authored the poem on page 21. Tanelle Garrison Bouchard wrote "Who Am I?" (page 151) when she was a teenage mother.

Anne DeWitt designed the cover around Michael Sawyer's photo. Photographer was one of his adoptive parents, Glen or Cherie Sawyer. "We were both snapping away that weekend, and we were too excited to notice who took which picture," Cherie commented. Michael's birthmother is also a lovely and courageous young woman.

Pam Patterson Morford's line drawings add some liveliness to the pages.

Steve Lindsay, Action Printing, Norman, Oklahoma, provided guidance in book design. I appreciate his expertise.

Carole Blum provided encouragement, many hours of typing, and other assistance.

Bob, as usual, was tolerant, supportive, and appreciative of my efforts. He's a delightful person and I love him.

TO MOM

By Jennifer Myers-Rick

Woman who cared, I thank you.
Woman who cared, I dream of you.
I feel us alike, you and I –
More alike than I ever dreamed.
I reach to tell you that I am
*   and that you would be proud.*
I reach to show you my life
*   but not to grab yours.*
I think I know the pain you felt;
I think I feel the love you gave.
You made the right choice.
Woman who cares, I thank you.

1

TO BE OR NOT TO BE –
A SCHOOL-AGE PARENT

Many women, including a lot of teenagers, have unplanned pregnancies. More than one million teenagers in the United States become pregnant each year. The majority of these pregnancies are unplanned.

Babies and sex perhaps should *not* be related. An 18-year dose of parenthood is a rather odd follow-up to ten or fifteen minutes of sex. But since the two – sex and babies – *are* very closely related, it is not surprising that so many of us experience unplanned, sometimes unwanted pregnancies.

Twenty-five years ago many pregnant teenagers relinquished (gave up, released, surrendered) their babies for adoption. An unmarried adolescent who became pregnant was often hustled off to Aunt Agatha's home in Missouri where she lived until her baby was born.

Usually the young mother didn't see her baby at all. It

was placed for adoption with a family she would never
meet. The entire event was wrapped in secrecy. Her friends
were told she was simply vacationing with Aunt Agatha.
She was urged to forget the whole episode and get back to
her "normal" life as a teenager.

Within the past twenty years, this picture has changed.
Women of all ages in the United States have a legal right to
an abortion during the early months of pregnancy. Each
year nearly 40 percent of those million teenage pregnancies
end in induced abortion. Perhaps 14 percent of the million
pregnancies end in spontaneous miscarriage.

But nearly 500,000 teenagers give birth each year. About
half are not married, and very few of these young women
relinquish their babies for adoption. About 2.5 percent
make informal adoption arrangements with relatives or
friends. Less than five percent go through the legal process
of releasing their infants for adoption. (1986: Project
SHARE. *The Adoption Option*)

School-age parents often have a
more difficult time parenting a
child than do older parents.

Technically, the word "relinquishment" refers to the
birthparents legally signing over (giving up) their child to
an adoption agency. The agency then places the child with
its adoptive family. Until the child is placed, the agency,
not the birthparents, has custody of the child. (See
Chapter Three.)

"Consent to adopt" is the term used to refer to birthparents legally releasing their child directly to its adoptive
parents as is done in independent adoption. (See
Chapter Five.)

Throughout this book, the terms "relinquish," "release," and "consent to adopt" are used interchangeably. Each refers to the legal act of releasing one's birthchild for adoption by another family.

Instead of these terms, many people prefer the phrase, "making an adoption plan." These words imply that the birthparents are involved in the adoption process. Some birthparents today choose the adoptive parents for their baby and remain in contact with them after the adoption is final. (See *Open Adoption: A Caring Option*, Morning Glory Press, 1987.)

Sometimes the term "natural parent" has been used to refer to the parent who gave birth to a baby, then released that baby for adoption. Some people feel this implies the adoptive parents must be "unnatural." To avoid this connotation, *birthparent* is the preferred term.

PARENTHOOD BY CHOICE?

If about 270,000 unmarried teenagers *choose* to keep their babies to rear themselves, their decision must be respected. It is possible for a young single mother to do a fine job of parenting, especially if she has a good support system within her family.

But is that choice consciously made? Or is becoming a mother often simply acceptance of what seems to be – that if one is pregnant and doesn't get an abortion, one will usually have a baby (true), and therefore raise that baby oneself (not necessarily true)?

Many young women are "successful" mothers. They give their children the care they need, sometimes at great sacrifice to themselves. They love their children deeply. But it is difficult to know who will be a good parent and who will not, whether that parent is single or married, 15 or 25 years

old. Some 25-year-old parents neglect their children. And sometimes a 15-year-old does a beautiful job of mothering.

Nevertheless, school-age parents often have a far more difficult time parenting a child (or children) than do older parents. Julie Gomoll, a young mother living in Portland, Oregon, wrote:

> *I remember being pregnant at 15. The only thing on my mind was that I wanted to keep my "baby."*
>
> *Sure, babies are easy to care for, needing only feeding, changing and hugs, but now I have a three-year-old son, a roommate, and someone who needs respect. Unlike a baby, he needs to share most of the decisions concerning him. When I have to be at a meeting or go to a class, my son must be interested in going to daycare too.*
>
> *Performing the tasks of a parent is not always*

rewarding and enjoyable. People get into parenting with little information on what it takes. I wanted to be a mom so that I could be on my own.

Somehow, becoming a teenager flipped a switch for me. That little taste of freedom: being able to stay out until 10 p.m., to go to parties and on dates was exciting. But I wanted more. I did not want to answer to anyone – not my folks, not my yelling and screaming brothers and sisters, and not my teachers. When my pregnancy test came back positive, it was my magical chance to be my own family. I could be my own boss.

Well, I've been my own boss for over two years now and it's scary. When I'm late for work, I can't blame it on my mom for not waking me. When my term paper isn't finished, I can't make my folks babysit all night – so I can't do it. I hate responsibility. Freedom has turned out to be something different than what I bargained for. What I did bargain for were all the goodies and none of the work.

I don't recommend motherhood as the way to independence.

POSSIBLE RESULTS
OF EARLY PREGNANCY

Extra problems for teenagers often start during pregnancy. Adolescents are much more likely to have toxemia and/or anemia during pregnancy than are older women. Both are serious health problems. Teenage mothers' babies are more likely to be premature and to be too small at birth. Other health problems may occur, often the result of poor nutrition, lack of prenatal care, or simply because of the physical immaturity of the young woman.

The majority of teenage mothers never finish high school. Most have no chance to obtain job skills or work experience. Three-quarters of all single mothers under 25 live in poverty. (1986: Children's Defense Fund. "Adolescent Pregnancy: Whose Problem Is It?")

The mere fact of becoming a mother before age 18 generally means a woman will be at least one step lower on the socio-economic ladder than she would be if she delayed parenting until she is in her 20s. That is, she is much more likely to be poor than is the woman whose first child is born later.

Julie continues:

> *I feel sad, angry, frustrated, and selfish when I think I brought a child of mine into the world when I was financially unstable, had no career goals, and no job experience. And because of these reasons, I was not emotionally ready to be a mom.*
>
> *In three years I had to learn to cook, do laundry and keep house, including learning how to keep budgets, balance a checking account, pay the utility bills, find good babysitters and afford them, not to mention finding beds, cribs, chairs, tables, pots, skillets, forks, knives, spoons, baby clothes, blocks, chalk boards, and everything else.*
>
> *I had to learn to drive, shop for food, find a job, decide on a career, and then find out how I could manage establishing that career.*
>
> *I had to and am still learning how to handle the system – welfare and its workers, employers, taxes, HUD, etc. Going to school, being a mom, and working is so much harder than I anticipated way back when, and I live it every day. I had no idea how hard it would be to parent.*

MARRIAGE OFTEN NO SOLUTION

"Majority of Teen Births Now Out-of-Wedlock" scream the headlines. Many of the newspaper and magazine stories devoted to teenage pregnancy are written as if the problem exists because less than half of these young parents are married. Of course this often means the father of the baby provides little if any financial support.

But "out-of-wedlock" may well be a healthy trend (compared to too-early marriage) – healthy from the standpoint of people coping with pregnancy and parenthood.

Most teenage marriages do not last long enough to solve the problems of too-early parenting. Brides who marry before they are 18 are four times as likely to have their marriages break up later as are women who marry in their early 20s. In fact, the majority of pregnant teen brides are divorced within six years.

If she marries the father of
her baby, she is far more
likely to drop out of school.

The reality is that few teenage males, whether married or not, can find jobs today which pay enough to support a family. In some areas, four out of five teenage men can find no job at all. Even with a high school diploma, the career of his dreams may take years of further education and experience before he can provide for a family.

If she marries the father of her baby, the young woman is far more likely to drop out of school after the birth of her child. Sometimes she does so at the insistence of her husband. Recently a 16-year-old called to say she wouldn't be returning to school after her baby's birth. "My husband says I have enough education to keep house," she explained.

The young woman who is married probably won't go to work if her husband is working. She may have another baby within a year. Few single mothers in our class have a repeat pregnancy before they marry and want another baby.

Yet five years later this married student has a high risk of being single again. If she is, she may have no high school diploma, no job skills, and must support and care for not just one, but two or even three small children.

When Brenda called about enrolling in the special class for pregnant students, she said she and her boyfriend were going to be married. She had dropped out of school a couple of months earlier because of her pregnancy. She had heard of the class, and thought perhaps she could earn her diploma before delivery.

Brenda's pregnancy was hard on her. She often missed school that winter, and she moved in with Manuel soon after their baby was born. Brenda explained:

All I could think about was how great it would be to get married. I thought we were madly in love and that marriage would solve everything. Manuel got a job and we set our wedding date. When Stacey was three months old, we got married.

I didn't know it yet, but I was pregnant again on my wedding day. And that was the pregnancy I didn't want to tell anyone about! I felt rotten again and Stacey took a lot of time. The apartment was always a mess, and we didn't have enough money.

Manuel lost his job the week after the doctor told me I was pregnant. We got unemployment for awhile, but he didn't find work. I don't think he tried very hard. He started laying around the apartment all day – I thought I'd go crazy!

The unemployment ran out so we had to go back on

welfare. And I had thought marriage would mean no more welfare. We were kicked out of one apartment because we couldn't pay the rent – and that was because welfare made a mistake and we didn't get our check on time.

We couldn't get our apartment back. We found another one, in a worse part of town.

She stressed that marriage doesn't solve everything.

Meghan was born two days after Christmas. I went home to my mother's for a couple of weeks. I couldn't have made it otherwise. Then I went back to our apartment with the two kids. Manuel got a job, but it lasted only a month. We were back on welfare.

This dragged on for almost a year. I would tell Manuel to leave. Sometimes he'd go, but he'd be back within a day or two. Finally I told him I was through. By then my nerves were shot. I went back to my mother's, and she said she'd keep the kids for awhile until I got myself together.

It was at this point that Brenda turned up at school again. She had decided she had to have her high school diploma and some job skills. She was already 19, so she wasn't admitted back into the high school. She started working on her remaining academic requirements in the Adult School Learning Lab. She spent the rest of her time in the Office Occupations Center learning secretarial skills.

One day she volunteered to talk to the Teen Mother Program students. She told her story, and stressed that marriage doesn't solve everything. "I thought I was so lucky because I could get married," she said wryly, "and now look at me – two kids and not even a high school diploma."

But Brenda's story has a happy ending – rather, beginning. She called a few months later to announce elatedly, "I have a job. I start Monday morning, and it pays pretty well. I think the kids and I can move into our own apartment in a month or so."

The following semester she took time off from work to speak to the new group of girls in class. She discussed the dangers in getting married because of pregnancy, then went on to speak enthusiastically about the need for a diploma and job skills, and of the satisfaction she's getting from working to support her two little girls. "It's hard work, and we still don't have much money," she concluded. "But we're a family again, the three of us, and I much prefer it this way."

"Will you get married again?" a student asked.

"Probably, if the right man comes along," she answered. "But I'll never marry again because I think I 'have' to."

The high school mother who remains single, continues her education and obtains job skills, is likely to be in a much better position three or four years later than is her formerly-married classmate. No wonder so many teenagers decide pregnancy is not enough reason to get married.

WHO IS MY MOTHER?

If a young single mother has the support of her family, she is usually better off than is the young woman completely on her own. However, this, too, can become a difficult situation.

Anita, who released her daughter for adoption two years ago, spoke of her concern for her friend, Claudia, and for Claudia's daughter, Nichole:

Claudia and I are almost the same age. She came into the Teen Mother Program a few weeks after I did, and we've been good friends ever since. The way I see her today and the way I see me is that I made the best choice. I only hope she feels she did the right thing for her.

Her baby is never with her – Claudia is never home. Nichole hardly knows who her mother is because her grandmother takes care of her. About the only time they're together is at night when the baby sleeps in Claudia's room.

Claudia is one of my best friends, yet she never brings Nichole with her when she comes over. And Nichole isn't a little brat, she's a neat little girl.

Claudia says, "Nichole hardly ever listens to me. She listens to my mother." Yet Claudia's here until 10 or 11 p.m. While I like to see her, I'd think she'd want to be with her daughter. But then she's young.

When Claudia thought about moving in with her sister, she said she wanted to move in without Nichole. She said, "I go to school, I go to work, then I go home. I'm too tired to face taking care of Nichole. My folks

scream at me and it's so bad sometimes I just leave."
    *I told her that when she does leave with Nichole, it
will break her parents' hearts, and she agreed. Her
Dad absolutely idolizes Nichole.*
    *I think we're alike in a lot of ways. I hope I would
have taken more of the responsibility if I had kept
Elizabeth. Claudia really isn't. She's giving the responsibility to her mother and dad. There's no way
I would expect my parents to take care of my child.*

Having, caring for, and loving children are joyful situations for many people. It is an especially joyful happening
if the timing is "right." Parenthood at 17 – or even 15 –
may be right for some people. But postponing parenthood
for a few years might make it more joyful for some of those
many teenagers – and older women with unplanned pregnancies – who each year keep their babies to rear themselves.
    Adoption is an option!

2

ARE YOU READY FOR PARENTHOOD?

How would you feel if you were a pregnant teenager? Or if your girlfriend were pregnant? Or you were an older woman facing an unplanned pregnancy alone?

Or . . . if you are pregnant now, how do you really feel about parenting a child? Do you think you have a choice *now* between being or not being a mother?

Assuming you have decided not to have an abortion, do you think any discussion of whether or not to parent a child concerns you? Do you still have options?

Perhaps your friends and/or your parents simply assume that because you're pregnant, you're going to have a baby to raise. Suzanne, a pregnant 16-year-old, wrote:

I wanted to get an abortion but I didn't have the money. Now that I'm this far along, I just have to take what Mother Nature gave me and treat it right.

*Before I got pregnant, I planned to be an actress
and marry a doctor. But now Kent can't go to medical
school, and I'm not even sure I'll be able to go to
college to study drama. If I had one wish, I'd wish I
could start my life over beginning at age 15. I would
rather have a baby when my career allows it.*

Suzanne doesn't believe she has a choice. For her,
motherhood *must* follow pregnancy.

Some teenagers' feelings about abortion versus adoption
are interesting. One girl said, "No, I would never give my
baby up for adoption. In my opinion, if others want to do
that, they should have an abortion instead of giving the
baby away to a stranger."

I have talked with several girls agonizing over the abortion decision. Jeanette told me she really didn't want to
have a baby because she had seen two of her sisters "ruin
their lives" (her words) by having babies when they were
15 or 16. She didn't want to be like them. But she also
explained that she considered abortion wrong, that she
thought of it as murder.

When adoption was mentioned as another option, she
quickly said, "Oh, no. If I go through the nine months of
pregnancy, I certainly won't give the baby away." Jeanette
finally decided to have an abortion.

I respect her right to that abortion. But I do question a
value system which says abortion is better than letting
another family rear that baby. So many couples desperately
want a baby but can't give birth to their own – couples who
probably would be able to give an adopted child a tremendous amount of love and care.

Today birthparents in many areas of the United States
and Canada can choose the adoptive family for their baby.
No longer do they have to "give the baby away" and never
see their child again if they make an adoption plan. For

some, this kind of "open" adoption makes an adoption decision more possible.

QUESTIONS TO PONDER

Many pregnant teenagers choose *not* to have an abortion. In fact, the majority of pregnant adolescents continue their pregnancies. So how do girls (and their boyfriends) make the heavy decision of whether to raise their babies themselves or place them for adoption? Is it usually an emotional decision – "I would *never* give my baby up for adoption"?

Or, as Diana put it, "I knew right away I would keep it. It's part of me. At first I thought I could release him for adoption, but then I thought I couldn't stand knowing I have a baby out there somewhere."

These are emotional decisions, but they show the extreme importance of the mother's feelings. Of course these feelings must be seriously considered. Good parenting, however, includes more than feelings.

Loving your baby is crucial, perhaps the most crucial aspect of parenting. But having enough money to feed him/her, living in a place you consider OK for both of you, being able to provide medical care for you and your baby – these unexciting things are also important.

There are other questions to consider. Do you think it's necessary for a child to have a father as well as a mother?

What about *you*? Can you continue your education if you're responsible for a child? Can you prepare for the kind of job you want?

Are you willing to give up a great deal of time to care for your child? Are you planning how you can take most of this responsibility, or are you expecting someone else to do much of the work?

Close your eyes and think of yourself as the mother

(or father) of a two-year-
old who is extremely lively
and says "No" a great deal.
How do you feel about
parenting a toddler who
often does his own thing?
Toddlers are quite different
from the infant who, while
she needs lots of cuddling
and physical care, sleeps a
lot and doesn't really
defy you.

   Still with your eyes
closed, think about your
child. Is she usually a
baby? Or do you anticipate
the toddler and preschool stages? Think about her going to
kindergarten. How old will you be then? Will you be ready
to be a room-mother at school?

   Surely most people don't think having a baby is punish-
ment. However, it is sometimes suggested that if a girl gets
pregnant, she should pay for her "wrongdoing" by raising
the baby.

   A student once said, "I will never give my baby up for
adoption. I made a mistake and I'm going to live with my
mistake."

   Kirsten, however, discusses in Chapter Five why she has
an entirely opposite opinion. She feels that placing a baby
with adoptive parents who want him very much is one way,
as she puts it, of "turning something bad into something
wonderful."

BETH'S FAMILY TODAY

   Beth was pregnant several years ago when she was a
high school senior. Recently I visited her. Obviously she is

enjoying her two children, her husband, and her home. When Eddie was born, Beth and Scott were ready for parenthood.

Eddie, barely 3, and Shannon, 1, were asleep when I arrived. About 15 minutes later Shannon toddled out. She smiled broadly as she gestured toward the cookie jar. Her mother changed her diaper, then handed her a cookie.

A few minutes later Eddie wandered out looking like a thundercloud. "He wakes up slowly just like me," his mother commented. After a brief rest on his mother's lap, he, too, was ready for a cookie. Then the two blonde, blue-eyed children went out to play in the warm California sunshine.

Beth chatted about her children ("They're into every-thing now!") and about Scott. They celebrated their fourth wedding anniversary last month, and she reported proudly that he was recently promoted to a better job. "We think we can afford a new car soon," she added with a smile.

We heard a commotion in the kitchen. Beth went in to check. I heard her exclaim, "Is Shannon in *there*?" She laughed and called me. She and Eddie were standing by a little cupboard but Shannon wasn't in sight. Eddie giggled as he opened the door of their toy cupboard. There was tiny Shannon, curled up on the second shelf. She had crammed herself into a space about eight inches high and perhaps two feet wide. She, too, giggled as she climbed out of her hiding place.

Obviously Beth, who was 22 in April, and Scott have a highly satisfying life with their children.

Five years ago Beth gave birth to another child, a little boy. She talked about that pregnancy and her difficult decision to place him for adoption:

It was the week after my 16th birthday that I real-ized I might be pregnant. I tried to ignore the whole

*idea, but as time went on, I knew it was true. I was
pregnant. I was scared to say anything to anybody.*

"The next morning she said,
'You're pregnant, aren't you?'"

---

*I was at least four months pregnant before I even
told Sam. We were still dating, but I knew things
weren't going to work out between us. He told me I
should get an abortion – he even offered to pay for it –
but it was too late for the suction method. Besides, I
didn't feel right about that.*

*So I wore baggy clothes and hoped no one would
notice. A couple of months later – I must have been at
least six months pregnant – my mom got a good side
view of me as I was going out one evening. The next
morning she said, "You're pregnant, aren't you?"*

*I said, "No." I just couldn't tell her or my father
because I knew it would kill them.*

"Well, I know you are," she replied.

*So she cried and I cried. Then she made an appoint-
ment for me to see our doctor.*

BETH CHANGES SCHOOLS

*I told her I didn't want to continue school where I
was, but neither did I want to go to the special school
in our district. It had a pretty bad reputation. After a
lot of discussion with her and my dad, we decided to
talk with our close friends, Alice and Bob, who had
recently moved from our neighborhood to a new home
about 80 miles away. I used to babysit for them.*

*Alice and Bob told us they had heard about a good
school program for pregnant students in their district.*

They suggested I enroll in this school and live with them until I delivered. So I moved in with them the next week. My mom told my friends I was visiting my cousin in Arizona. Surprisingly, we pulled it off. Most of my friends never knew I was pregnant.

"When did you decide to release the baby for adoption?"

My folks kind of influenced me at first. They didn't tell me what to do, but my mom said, "You're going to release it for adoption, aren't you?"

So I said, "Well, yes, whatever you want." I had found out I was still alive after telling them I was pregnant, and I wasn't going to push my luck right then. But as I thought about it, it sounded like a good idea. I wanted to finish high school, perhaps go on to college. I just didn't think it would work with a baby.

It was purely my decision. I knew that in our family I really couldn't raise the baby and do what I wanted to do. I did ask my mom how she would feel if I kept it. She told me she would love the baby, but she would not raise it. She said if I needed a babysitter, I would have to find someone else. I knew she meant it.

By then, I really knew inside that I was going to relinquish for adoption, but I wanted to find out how they might feel if I did decide to keep it.

My dad had told me I didn't have to move in with Alice and Bob. He told me if my friends were nasty to me, they weren't good friends anyhow. But I wanted to go there. I still think it was the right thing to do.

I lived with Alice and Bob and attended the special school for about three months. I felt pretty good most of the time so I helped Alice take care of their two little boys. I also learned to cook – something I hadn't done at home much.

One cold night early in March I went into labor. My little boy was born late the next afternoon. The doctor didn't think I should see my baby. But I insisted, and of course they let me. He was beautiful.

"Of course it's hard giving up a baby you've carried for nine months, but life goes on."

"Have you ever regretted your decision?"

No, I haven't. I suppose I could if I thought a lot about it. Of course I think about him, but I have my family now and he has his. He'll start kindergarten this fall. I do wish I knew what he looks like, if he has many friends, how his parents treat him.

If I were making an adoption plan today I understand I could meet the adoptive parents and actually have a continuing relationship if we wanted to. That wasn't possible when I released my baby.

Adoption is a big deal. But I think maybe it isn't as big a deal as some girls think it is. Of course it's hard giving up a baby you've carried for nine months. But life goes on. I think about him every now and then, but I don't let it get to me.

ROBIN DECIDES TO PARENT

That same day I visited with another young mother. Robin is 19 and her son, Stu, is 3. Robin, who became pregnant at 15, talked to an adoption counselor. She decided, however, to keep her baby. She, too, knows she made the right decision – for her.

Robin is living in a city about 40 miles from my home.

When I phoned her, she suggested we meet for lunch at
her favorite restaurant. She had spoken enthusiastically
of her new job selling real estate. She said her time was
her own and she could see me for as long as we liked.

Robin was waiting when I walked in – even more
lovely, taller, and slimmer than I remembered. As we ate
pizza, she talked about her life during the past two years, a
time when I had seen her only occasionally. Stu was born
while Robin was in tenth grade. He stayed in the Infant
Center on campus while his mother worked furiously on
her high school graduation requirements. And she made it –
a year early.

---

*"It wasn't anything new to
me to change a diaper, to
hold, to cuddle."*

Soon after Robin's graduation she and her family moved
to their present home a couple of miles outside the city. She
had attended the community college these past two years.
She had also earned her realtor's license.

For a brief time last year Robin and Stu lived with a
young man. That didn't work out so they came back home.
She reminisced:

*Living away those few months made a difference in
my relationship with my mom. I loved having my own
place, being on my own. We had a tight budget, and I
learned a lot – cooking, cleaning, managing. I did
enjoy it, but I had moved in with Abe more for conven-
ience – to get away from home – than for love. And
that doesn't work.*

*So I came back home. Now my mom knows I can
make it on my own, that I'm not a child. That's made a*

big difference in our relationship. We get along better now than we ever did before.

"What's it really like, being the single mother of a three-year-old son?"

Stu has been a joy. He talks at least a mile a minute. Would you believe he and I sit around and just chat? We can have a conversation for 45 minutes! How many mothers can do that with a three-year-old? He's very smart, a little mature for his age, I think. He has never known what it's like having a father and he has adjusted well.

It's neat having him around. I don't feel he has been a hindrance in my life, perhaps because I haven't known anything else for so long.

Maybe he does put a damper on my social life, but then I hang around mostly with people who enjoy Stu, and he usually goes along with me. We go camping and do lots of things together. My mother takes care of him while I work, but she seldom does any other time. We both know babysitting Stu isn't her responsibility. It's entirely mine.

"How did you feel about being pregnant?"
Fat! I knew I was pregnant two weeks after I conceived. I told the baby's father about a week later.
"Well, you can do one of two things," he said.
"Oh?" I replied.
"Yes, you can either get an abortion or you can marry me."
"Marry you? Sorry," I said. He vanished soon after that. I think he's in the service now, but I'll never press charges. I don't need him. Physically he is Stu's father, but mentally, no."

HER PARENTS' REACTION

I didn't tell my parents until I couldn't fit into my clothes any longer. By then, I was about five months pregnant. My mother cried, thought it was her fault. I kept saying, "How can it be your fault? I'm the one who screwed around!"

Since my aunt works in an adoption agency, naturally my mother made an appointment for me to talk to a counselor there. I talked with the worker (not my aunt) for nearly two hours.

She told me that a lot of unwed mothers my age keep their babies at first, then relinquish them later because they can't cope — like two years down the road they give them up.

I took it all in. I listened and then I said, "OK, but I have made my decision."

When I told her I was going to keep the baby, she said I should go home and think about it. But I had

*already decided. I kept him — because I'm headstrong
and because I'm me! I don't regret my decision.*

*When I brought him home from the hospital, of
course it was hard work taking care of him. But I was
expecting that. I'm the oldest in a family of five
children.*

*I was my littlest brother's mother, practically. It
wasn't anything new to me to change a diaper, to
hold, to cuddle. Perhaps that's why I didn't worry and
think, "Oh, my God, how will I do this?" I had already had a lot of responsibility. My mother would
have gone nuts if I hadn't helped her with my little
brothers.*

*What always fascinated and awed me was that this
baby was an extension of myself. I could help form
him into the kind of person I wanted him to be, caring,
happy, able to go through anything and come out all
right.*

*Thinking about all that responsibility didn't scare
me. It awed me. It's a whole new thing — having a new
baby means he's totally dependent on you for his life!*

*Parenting Stu didn't work well because of good
luck. It worked well because I made it. I worked — and
am working — hard at being a good parent.*

Enthusiastic as Robin is about motherhood, she is
absolutely sure she doesn't want another child. In fact, she
is so sure that she recently had a tubal ligation (operation
which should make it impossible for her to become pregnant again). She explained:

*I know I'm doing a good job parenting Stu. I'm
happy with my life, but I also know a second child
would complicate things. Even if/when I marry, I don't
want another child.*

ERIN'S LIFE

Not all young mothers feel as positive about early motherhood as Robin does. Erin's lovely Joanna is almost two years old. Joanna has been coming to "school" at the Infant Center since two weeks after her birth. Erin will graduate soon. She then plans to continue her education and become a teacher.

"Everybody wanted to babysit for me at first, but when she was seven or eight months old, they lost interest in her."

Erin, who obviously loves Joanna dearly and does an excellent job of mothering her little daughter, discussed her experiences recently:

I wish I had been married and had waited longer to get pregnant. It's awfully hard raising her by myself.

It's harder as she gets older. When she was born, she was fussed over by my mother and my grandmother. They helped a lot at first. So did my friends. Everybody wanted to babysit, but by the time she was seven or eight months old, they lost interest in her. Most of my friends quit coming to my house after that. I guess Joanna got too old for them.

When I was pregnant, I thought my mother would help more than she does. It's been worse than I expected. I take care of my little sister a lot on weekends, but my mom almost never babysits Joanna. I either have to take her with me wherever I go or stay home.

During the past week Joanna hasn't been napping at all during the day. She's awake all day long, she's cutting her molars, and she's very fussy.

As she gets older, she's harder to handle. She throws temper tantrums, and when she gets really frustrated, she bites. Sometimes I get so tired I think I'll drop.

"What do you see ahead for yourself?"

Hopefully I'll get my education and be a teacher. When Joanna graduates from the Infant Center when she's two, I can put her in the other Children's Center here in the district while I go on to school.

I would like to get married, but if I do, I will still go ahead with my education. I couldn't sit home and take care of a house all day long.

"Do you have any advice for a young, pregnant teenager, or for an older pregnant woman, perhaps single, who didn't plan to have a baby now??"

First I would ask her what she thinks she wants to do with the rest of her life. Then I would tell her how hard it is to have a baby and still try to do what you want. We have childcare here at school, and still it's hard. It must be really bad if you don't have that. I would remind her how important it is to go to school.

Then I'd ask, "Do you want the baby or not?" If she's already five months pregnant, I'd tell her she has only two options: give the baby up, or keep it and take care of it.

CONSIDER ALL OPTIONS

If you are young and pregnant, think about the good and the not-so-good things about early parenthood. To help your thinking, write down the good and the bad things about each possible choice. Each pregnant girl who has

decided against abortion still has at least two choices –
keeping the baby versus placing him for adoption. Some
young women can also choose between staying single and
getting married.

Mark either two or three columns on a sheet of paper,
depending on how many choices you have. Now write
down all the good things about raising a child – whether
you're single or are/might be married. In another column
write down the good things about not having a baby to care
for at this point in your life.

On a second sheet of paper, jot down the things you
don't like about each of your possible choices.

Now, which choice seems to have more positive things
going for you?

While you're pregnant you can't make a legally binding
decision to release your baby for adoption. According to

law, you must wait until after delivery to sign relinquishment papers. But it's important to consider all your options
long before that time.

The following comments come from teenagers who had
to make decisions concerning early unplanned pregnancy.
Sally, while she was still pregnant, commented:

*At first I was scared, but now I'm happy about
having a baby. My parents wanted me to get an
abortion. Then they pushed adoption, but I wouldn't
consider either one.*

*I'm worried whether or not I can provide a good
life for the baby. It makes me unhappy, though, the
way everyone lectures me. They say I'm stupid for
ruining my life. I decided to have the baby regardless
of what my parents think or what anyone else says.*

*When everything is going right and I feel up, I'm
happy. I just hope I can still have my freedom after the
baby is born.*

Sue, an 18-year-old with a two-year-old child, suggests:

*Well, I think if you're really ready to have a child,
that's neat. But you should think of the things you
have to give up, especially if you're single. With a
baby you can't always do the things you're used to
doing. Sometimes things can get to you after awhile.*

A young woman who made an adoption plan for her
child writes:

*If you're pregnant, please consider your future and
your baby's – consider adoption. I released my little
girl two years ago when she was born – and I'm glad
I did.*

Diana, who doesn't feel she has had a chance to consider her options, explains:

When I was pregnant, I thought my relationship with Jim would last. I didn't think about adoption until Tina was about five months old. I wanted to (consider adoption) really bad by then, but I didn't have anybody to talk to about it. I didn't know what to do.

A baby needs parents that are a little older and ready to settle down. They can do more things with her and spend more time with her. Now, me, I still want to go out. There is so much out there that I want to do and see.

I tried to talk to my mom, but she said, "How could you do that?" She is so afraid of what people might think. But I think it would be better for Tina to have two parents.

Shawna, who is the 19-year-old mother of two children and is married to the father of her second baby, said:

Having children at a young age is very satisfying to me, but sometimes I wish I had waited. I love my children and I wouldn't give them up for anything.

But I don't advise anyone who has big plans to get pregnant too young because your child should always come first. If you have plans for the future, sometimes you can't spend enough time with your kids.

AM I READY TO BE A PARENT?

Chapter 13 contains some questions. Answering these questions thoughtfully and honestly may help you decide whether you are ready to parent at this point in your life.

The questions are meant simply to give you ideas to think about. Of course there are no "right" answers and no grades.

The questionnaire can help an unmarried pregnant woman or a couple expecting a baby to sort out their feelings concerning keeping the child or releasing him/her for adoption (or having an abortion, if time permits).

The same questionnaire is, of course, also helpful for couples who aren't yet expecting a child. Almost everyone would agree that it is much easier for such a couple to decide not to have children now than it is for the woman who is already pregnant.

*But even if you're pregnant now, you, too, have that choice.*You don't need to parent until *you* feel you're ready. Adoption *is* an option.

3

HOW ADOPTION WORKS – AGENCIES

Many young women unintentionally pregnant talk to adoption agency counselors simply because they want to talk to someone. They may not plan to place their babies for adoption, but they know a counselor can help them sort out their feelings and concerns.

If you're worried about an unplanned pregnancy, or you aren't quite sure of your decision regarding your child's future, you can talk things over with a trained counselor. Look in the yellow pages of your telephone book under "Adoption." You'll probably find one or more listings if you live in an urban area. You can also contact your state or local child welfare agency for information.

Two kinds of adoption services are available – agency and independent. Independent adoption, in which the birthparents place their baby directly with adoptive parents, will be discussed in Chapter Five.

If you contact an adoption counselor, s/he will help you think through *your* situation. Even if you're sure you want to release your baby for adoption, s/he will help you think carefully of all alternatives before making a final decision.

"Pat never did try to talk me
into adoption – she just wanted
to help me find out what would
be best for me."

In agency adoption, birthparents relinquish (surrender, release) their child to the adoption agency. The agency then places the child with a carefully selected family. In some agency adoptions, the birthparents never meet the adoptive parents. Birthparents don't know their baby's new parents' names, nor do the adoptive parents know theirs.

Birthparents who deal with an agency, however, usually have some choice in the family who will receive their child. They may not know the family's identity, but their case-worker will describe one, usually several, would-be adoptive families.

These are families already approved for placement of a child by the agency, families which the agency thinks would be suitable for this particular baby. The birthmother – and father, if he is involved – may then choose the family she/they prefer for the baby.

More and more adoption agencies are allowing, even encouraging some degree of openness in adoption. Often the birthparents and adoptive parents exchange letters, perhaps pictures. They may meet once without exchanging last names and addresses. Sometimes they may exchange full identification and continue a relationship with each other as the child grows up.

Jennifer Stebbins, M.S.W., Pregnancy Counselor, Christian Adoption and Family Service, Anaheim,

California, is a strong advocate of open adoption. "We don't encourage a young mother to place her child blindly," she explained. "Sometimes a young woman feels other people think an adoption plan means abandoning her child.

"If she has made a concrete plan – she has chosen her baby's adoptive parents – and she knows that plan came out of the love she feels for her baby, she knows this is entirely opposite from abandonment. Through the letters and pictures she receives from the adoptive parents, she *knows* her child has a wonderful loving family."

If you would like to meet the family planning to adopt your child, discuss your wishes with your counselor. For more information on "open" adoption, see *Open Adoption: A Caring Option.*

HELP FROM LISA'S COUNSELOR

Lisa, a lovely dark-haired senior, knew she wanted to go to college and have a career. Could she cope with motherhood at 17 and still continue with her plans? She decided to talk to a counselor at Children's Home Society, a large adoption agency. She relates her story:

I almost didn't call Pat (the agency caseworker) because I thought someone from an adoption agency

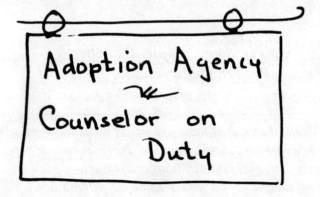

*would want to talk to me just for my kid – that she'd
try to con me into giving my baby up and signing the
paper as fast as possible. I'd even heard adoption
agencies referred to as baby-stealers, but she wasn't
like that at all.*

*Pat never did try to talk me into adoption – she just
wanted to help me find out what would be best for me.*

*You see, I tried to ignore my pregnancy for at least
six months. I didn't believe it at first – I kept going to
school and ignoring the whole thing. By four months I
had to admit this had happened, but I told only two
friends in the next couple of months. I kept wearing my
coat to school so no one else would know. I wasn't
with the father any longer and I was pretty miserable.*

*Finally my parents found out. They were really
understanding – I had thought they'd about kill me.
Instead, my mother simply said, "Well, we'll have to
take you to the doctor tomorrow."*

*At first my mother assumed I was going to keep the
baby. But when I started talking to Pat, Mom apparently thought it would be better for me to give it up.
She didn't say so, but I could tell by the things she did
say like "What are you going to do?" and "How will
you support it?" I was about a semester away from
high school graduation and I planned to go on to
college.*

---

*"For some people it's better to
keep the baby, and for others,
to give it up."*

---

*I talked to Pat at least five or six times during those
last two months. Sometimes we'd talk for two or three
hours about all kinds of things. Of course we talked
about adoption and what I could do without a kid.*

*I remember once I said I didn't think hardly anyone
who is real young could make it with a baby.*

*Pat told me that was not so – that for some people
it's better to keep the baby, and for others, to give it
up. She told me about different couples ready to adopt
a child, couples she thought might be right for my
baby if I decided on adoption.*

*I especially remember one couple – the man was
president of his company and the mother stayed home.
They had a big house and several horses. That would
have been nice for Stevie. Of course I know love is the
most important thing, but I would have liked him to
have money too.*

*When I was considering adoption, I worried that
when he learned he was adopted, he might hate me for
giving him up. Pat said a birthmother can write letters
to her child explaining her situation, and that some
adoptive parents are willing to keep in touch through
the years. If I had decided on adoption, I would have
wanted an arrangement like that.*

HER FRIENDS
OPPOSE ADOPTION

*I had only one friend who thought I should release
my baby. All the rest were against it. They would say,
"Oh God, how could you?" and "Don't even say
that, how could you think of giving it away?"*

*People in our class at school would talk about
another girl who was giving up her baby. They said,
"How can she do that after going through all that
pain?" I told them it takes more love to give a baby
up than to keep it.*

*A lot of girls don't consider adoption because they
worry about what other people think. I thought about*

*that, too. I did think about adoption, but never was
sure what I wanted to do. Then when he was born, my
mother brought me flowers. My friends came to see
me and the baby. It would have been terribly hard to
face them if I had decided to release him. It must be
awful at that point for girls who do.*

*But I kept him and I'm glad I did. My mother helps
me a lot, and my parents are willing to let me stay
here while I go on to school.*

*I want to be a dental hygienist. They make pretty
good money – that's one of the things I like about it.
But you can also pick your own hours. When I do get a
job, I'll be able to be home when Stevie comes home
from school. I'd like that because I could be here and
watch him grow.*

"Had you planned to be a dental hygienist before you
became pregnant?"

*I had thought about it a little, but I guess I had
always wanted something better, like being a veteri-
narian. I might still go to school at night later when
he's a little older. Perhaps I could become a dentist.
But I know I'll enjoy being a dental hygienist.*

"How has your life changed? How is this summer with a
four-month-old baby different from last summer?"

*Just going to the beach! I used to take only my
towel. Now I have a bassinet, diapers, food, sun
shade, extra clothes – and I go only once or twice a
week. Last year I went every day. I don't go by myself
either because I need a little help carrying everything.
But it's not that different. I do have to think ahead
more – I can't do things on the spur of the moment.*

But it's a nice change. The La Leche League

speaker (organization for women who breastfeed their babies) at school said breastfeeding is nice for the mother because she has to sit down and relax when she feeds her baby. She can't prop a bottle, then go on working furiously. I agree – and I'm enjoying relaxing with Stevie instead of always being on the go like I used to be.

I'm not dating right now – I don't want to, perhaps because I'm pretty busy – but I don't feel tied down with him. I can do just about anything I did before, as long as I include him in my plans.

It wasn't easy those first two months. When I first came home from the hospital, I thought I'd die! He wet about every 15 minutes, and I'm sure I didn't get even an hour's sleep those first two nights. I thought, "How long will this last?" Sometimes I thought about adoption again because those first two months were terrible.

But when he was two months and one week old, he started sleeping through the night. Now he usually wakes about 6 a.m. I put him in bed with me and nurse him. Then he goes back to sleep.

AGENCY SELECTS ADOPTIVE FAMILIES

Lisa's story matches the blurb in an agency brochure: "When you're pregnant and you're not married, it often seems that everybody's trying to tell you what to do. That's when Children's Home Society can help. We don't want to take over your life or tell you what you should do. We just want to help you make the best decisions possible for yourself and your child."

Agencies, which may be public or sectarian (church-related), usually select their adoptive families carefully. In fact, agencies have been highly criticized for being so selective. But if it were your baby they were placing, would you criticize their efforts at finding the best family possible?

Families who apply for a healthy baby through an agency generally must wait several years for "their" baby, according to Janice Wills, Child Welfare Worker, Los Angeles County Department of Children's Services.

"They may wait six or seven years for a normal healthy Caucasian infant. The wait for a healthy Hispanic baby is much shorter, and there may be no wait for a Black baby," she explained. "There are homes waiting for all babies, Hispanic, Black, mixed race. No healthy infant need wait for an adoptive home," she added.

Julia L. Richardson, Program Manager, Children's Home Society, Los Angeles, explained that her agency accepts adoptive parent applicants only two or three times a year as needed. "We do a short screening process and select couples who meet our needs at the present time," she said. "We are more likely to need couples interested in open adoption, people who may be willing to meet the baby's birthparents.

"Because we are not accepting many applicants now, those who are accepted may wait only a year, perhaps two, for a baby," she added. Statewide, Children's Home Society of California places about 450 babies per year, according to Ms. Richardson.

PREPARING ADOPTIVE PARENTS

Prospective adoptive parents usually attend a group meeting with other would-be parents. At this meeting they learn about the children waiting for adoption. They explore their own reasons for wanting to adopt a child. They also learn more about the process of adoption.

In many agencies, an important part of this group meeting involves adoptive parents meeting, talking with,

and hearing the stories of birthparents. Adoptive parents
who don't know any birthparents may not understand the
pain involved in releasing a child for adoption.

Sometimes adoptive parents fear the unknown birthparents, thinking they might return for their child. They
realize they won't be adopting the babies of the birthparents participating in the group meeting. However, simply
talking with birthparents helps a would-be adoptive couple
develop empathy for their future adoptive child's
birthparents.

After the adoptive couple fills out a lengthy application
form, an agency social worker meets with the couple
together and separately, and visits them in their home.
Topics discussed usually include the adoptive couple's reasons for wanting to adopt a child, the strength of their
marriage, their attitudes toward childrearing, their financial
stability, and their capabilities for parenting a child born to
someone else.

Basically, the agency is looking for the kind of parents you would like your child to have if you decide you want someone else to raise him/her. They want couples who have a stable home life where a child will fit in comfortably. Above all, they want a home where a child will feel wanted and loved.

"I'M GOING TO BE A DOCTOR"

Kathi's dream is to go to medical school. She has wanted to be a pediatrician for as long as she can remember. When she realized she was pregnant early in her sophomore year at a private school, she was horrified. At first, she told no one.

Later, when she faced her reality, she decided to check with an adoption agency. Being able to read descriptions, then choose from several adoptive families was important to her. She remembers:

I was scared but I blocked it out for two months. I probably seemed happy those two months because I pretended it wasn't real.

I finally told a couple of people because I knew I had to get help. Within two weeks they started telling other people and it was a horrible disaster.

My mom was suspicious, so she searched in my purse and found the paper that said I had a pregnancy test. It didn't say whether the test was positive or not so she asked me. I figured I'd better tell her and she got real mad.

"I didn't want to take her into my parents' home to live in my room. That's just not good."

She yelled and called my dad home from work. They thought it would be best if I got an abortion. They were real upset for a long time.

Two weeks after my parents found out, the principal and counselor at my school called me in. They never mentioned my pregnancy. They just told me I couldn't come to school any longer.

This was two weeks before Christmas vacation and I had expected to stay at least until then. But they called my mom and sent me home that day. It's a private school and they had never let girls stay while they're pregnant.

I thought they were wrong and so did my parents. But they wouldn't let me continue there. A year later, probably because of my parents' agitating, they changed that rule. Now a pregnant girl can stay if she wants, but that didn't help me.

I had checked out the special program for pregnant girls before I was kicked out. I didn't want to go there, mostly because my parents and I didn't think it had good enough college-prep classes. I couldn't get my advanced math or my French III there.

My public school district has a special school with very strong college-prep curriculum. You have to pass a test to qualify. During Christmas vacation I took the test, and two weeks later they said I could enroll. That was a good experience.

BABY'S FATHER NOT INVOLVED

The counselor at that school helped me a lot. She even gave me some special assignments on prenatal nutrition and other stuff dealing with pregnancy and decision-making.

When I was kicked out of my school, I wasn't sure

whether I would parent, but I probably knew in my
heart that I wouldn't. The father wasn't around even
then, and I didn't think I wanted to bring a baby into
that situation. I didn't know if he would be coming
back, if he cared, and I had to think of the baby's life.
I didn't want to take her into my parents' home to live
in my room. That's just not good.

I felt they were right
when I first saw the picture.

A baby needs to be brought up in a stable home
with parents who are married and are dedicated to
having that baby, someone who wants to be a parent
immediately. But that wasn't the case. I'm not old
enough, I'm not an adult, and children shouldn't
parent children. I'm not prepared and I'd not be able
to give her what she needs. I'd have to go to school
and I couldn't be with her – or I'd have to drop out of
school which would have been terrible for me.

The baby's father was around again during the last
two months of pregnancy, and he thought I should
keep the baby. But I couldn't be sure of his intentions.
He might skip out again and I had to think about that.

The best solution was that I go on with my life and
try to make the most of it, and at the same time, do the
best I could with her life.

I went to the adoption agency associated with our
church. The counselor was wonderful – we talked a
lot. She took La Maze classes with me and was my
coach during labor and delivery.

She showed me files from six adoptive couples. You
go through these files and read their thoughts on
discipline, their likes and dislikes, their hobbies,
occupation, why they want a child. You also see a
picture and a letter from them. I still have that letter.

I chose this couple because they're young and they like to do the same things as my family. They were flexible and they seemed excited. I felt they were right when I first saw the picture. The more pictures I get now, the more I can see I made a good choice.

I met them once but I don't know their name or where they live. They send me letters every once in awhile and let me know how my daughter is doing. I keep all of the letters and pictures in a big photo album.

I didn't sleep real well for a couple of weeks after I came home from the hospital, but I think the adoption was best. That's what keeps me going. If I didn't think it was best, I'd feel worse. It's best for her, and my life is moving forward. It's best for my sisters and my family, too. Rather than being sad, each day the sadness gets less and the happiness for her gets more – I'm happy for her, excited for her in her new life.

JENNIFER'S DILEMMA

Jennifer had a special request concerning the religion of her baby's adoptive parents. In fact, she switched agencies because of that special request:

I knew right away I was pregnant because when I have a period I'm right on the dot. I started eating better for the baby's sake, but I planned adoption because I knew I couldn't keep it – not when I was only 14 and in the ninth grade.

"Some girls seemed against me because I was giving my baby up. Sometimes I felt so bad."

For at least a month I didn't tell anybody. Then I told one friend that I was pregnant and was going to place the baby for adoption. She immediately said she would take it, but I said no. She agreed it was my decision.

During the next two or three months I told three other friends, and they didn't bug me – just said it was up to me. Of course I thought about getting an abortion, but I had always thought it was wrong so I didn't go that route.

By Christmas I started to show. Everybody began talking around school and I just couldn't handle it. My mother still didn't know. So right after the holidays I talked with my counselor. I hadn't even gotten a pregnancy test yet and I was at least five months pregnant. She told me about the special class for pregnant students and said I'd better get to the doctor real soon.

So that same day I visited the class and went to the hospital for a pregnancy check. That night I told my mother. All she said was, "How could you?" Of course she was upset, but she took it pretty good. She didn't talk much for three days, but she did sign the papers so I could enroll in the special class the next day. My new teacher thought I was quite efficient to get all that done in one day.

The class was fine except some of the girls seemed to be against me because I was giving my baby up. Sometimes I felt so bad. The worst day was when a girl said, "Are you still giving your baby away?" I said I was, and she replied, "You're a fool!"

I was furious, so I said, "Don't you ever call me a fool!" At that point one of the teachers told the girls that she had adopted her son, and it had worked out fine. They liked her a lot, so after that they pretty much let me alone.

I've always been strong, but while I was pregnant, I couldn't handle things so well. I would really feel hurt. Some of the girls were understanding. They'd say, "It's your decision, so don't worry about what anyone else thinks."

I couldn't stand comments on the other side either. While I was in the doctor's office waiting to have my blood pressure checked, I heard one nurse say to another, "Is she giving it up for adoption?"

When the other nurse said I was, the first one commented, "That's good. She's too young – she shouldn't keep it." I suppose I'm stubborn, but at that point I felt more like keeping my baby than at any other time.

First I talked to a counselor from a big agency. My mother wanted to be sure the baby was placed with a family with the same religion as ours. The first case-worker said she would try, but she couldn't promise. Then my mom heard about a smaller agency, one that works only with Christian families. Their social worker said they had a family waiting who belonged to a church like ours.

After I delivered, one nurse was especially nice to me. She got her baby through adoption, and she would come in and talk to me. When I was in labor, we got really close. She invited me over to her house, and I think I'll be babysitting for her. Her daughter is five years old now and she really loves her.

"I'm glad I did it this way.
I think about him but it's
getting easier as time goes by."

I wrote my baby a letter and sent him a little gift. The social worker said she would get it to him.

"How would you feel if your baby tried to find you later?"

I don't know how I'd react. I probably would be happy that he would want to know who I am. But I suppose it would depend partly on how much I've told my husband and other kids. I'd like to know he's OK.

I wouldn't go searching though. If he wants to find me, fine, but I wouldn't go out and look. That could be hard on him – all of a sudden to have me pop up and say, "Hello, I'm your mother!"

I'm glad I did it this way, but I do think about him. I was thinking this morning that next month he'll be two years old. It's getting easier as time goes by.

Any advice for other 14-year-olds?

Well, a 14-year-old isn't ready to be a mother – she's still growing up herself. Janeen (pregnant friend) cracks me up. She just turned 14 and she's going to keep her baby! But she's going to want to go out just as I did. And she's going to be leaving that baby with her mother a lot – or staying home.

I want to do so much – go to college and do something with my life. I want to grow up slowly – I didn't want suddenly to have to be mature. I wanted to take my time, and a baby wouldn't have fit in. Janeen will have to grow up quickly because a child needs a mother to look up to. She can't be playing games while the baby is, too. She'll have to be more mature.

I'm content with my decision.

4

MORE ABOUT
LEGAL MATTERS

If you decide to release your child for adoption, you cannot sign the final papers until *after* you leave the hospital. However, you will be asked to sign a release form in the hospital stating that someone else can take the baby away from there. If you release through an agency, this person will be a representative of that agency. This does *not* mean the birthmother or birthfather has signed away her/his rights to the child.

As soon as the birthmother and birthfather have signed the relinquishment papers, the baby can be placed in his permanent adoptive home. He will be in a foster home until these papers are completed. Sometimes, if both the birthmother and father have made their decision immediately after birth, the father can sign at once and the mother can complete this step on her way home from the hospital. If this happens, their baby can probably be placed with the

adoptive family immediately, a nice situation for any
new-born baby.

Relinquishment becomes "final and binding" (you can't
change your mind about giving up your child) when these
signed papers are filed by the agency with the State Department of Social Services. Once the birthparents have signed
the adoption papers and the adoption plan has been accepted by the State Department of Social Services, the
birthparents generally no longer have any legal rights or
responsibility for their child.

Not all states have the same laws regarding adoption,
however. A Uniform Adoption Act has been accepted by
some states but not all. If you decide to place your baby
through an adoption agency, the agency worker will inform
you of all the rights you have under the law in your state.

Some groups across the country are working toward a
change in this law. Some would like birthparents to have an
interval of time in which they could decide to keep their
child even after they have signed the adoption papers.

BABY HAS TWO
BIRTH CERTIFICATES

Jennifer completed the form for her baby's birth certificate while she was in the hospital. After the adoption was
finalized, a new birth certificate was issued. In this one, the
adoptive parents were listed as if the baby had been born
to them.

The first birth certificate, the one with Jennifer's and the
baby's biological father's names on it, was "sealed" – filed
away where it cannot be seen except by order of the court.

Secrecy has been part of most agency adoptions since the
1940s. If birthparents wanted to meet the adoptive parents,
they could choose independent adoption. Many people,
however, prefer to go through an agency because of the

careful checking they do with the adoptive families and because of the counseling they offer the birthparents. The agency acts as the birthparents' advocate.

Birthparents can sometimes
keep in touch with the adoptive family
through the agency.

In some states at this time, the law will not allow release of "sealed" adoption information. Neither the adoptee nor the birthparents can see the adoptee's original birth certificate. (See Chapter 11 for accounts of birthparents and adoptees who searched for and found each other.)

INFORMATION REQUIREMENT ACT

Several years ago in California, the Information Requirement Act was passed. According to this Act, when the adoptee is 21, s/he can obtain the name and address of his/her birthparents IF permission is on file from the birthparents to release this information.

"We ask birthparents to sign a form which explains the Information Requirement Act," commented Janice Wills, Los Angeles County Department of Adoptions. "We ask them to let us know when they have health problems which might affect the child. We also ask that they keep us up to date on their addresses.

"The birthparent may state on this form that her birthchild may contact her later if s/he wishes to do so. The birthparent can change her mind at any time in the future by sending a notarized letter by registered mail to the agency. That is, if she originally said she did not want to be contacted, she may at a later date give her permission for her child to do so. Or she may withdraw that permission if she wishes," Ms. Wills concluded.

Birthparents can sometimes keep in touch with the adoptive family through the agency caseworker. Birthparents occasionally write to their worker, perhaps years later, with information to share with their child. Adoptive parents can also give the caseworker information about their child to share with the birthparents.

Perhaps you know you don't want to "give your baby to strangers," but you might be interested in adoption if you could meet the adoptive parents. You'd like to satisfy yourself that they are the kind of people you want to parent your child. Discuss your wishes with your caseworker. If that agency doesn't permit such a plan yet, perhaps another agency in your area will.

Meeting the adoptive parents does not, of course, change the finality of actual relinquishment. "Relinquishment" means a legal document has been signed by the birthparents and they no longer have legal rights or responsibility for their child.

JODIE'S DECISION

Jodie assumed she would keep her child. But, when she was about six months pregnant, she began thinking more and more about the realities of mothering, of the tremendous changes a baby would bring into her life.

Jodie was president of the youth group at her church, an eleventh grader everyone looked up to. If anyone else had a problem, her pastor would say, "Go see Jodie."

She was 16 and dating a 20-year-old. They had sex only once. Two weeks later in early April she told Tim she thought she was pregnant. Her periods had always been completely regular, but he told her she was just worried . . . that of course she wasn't pregnant after only one time.

A week or two later she told him again, and once more he assured her it was because she was worried about it, and that she really wasn't pregnant.

When they realized she was, he said, "I'll do whatever you want – pay for an abortion, marry you . . ." But her feelings made abortion an impossible choice. As for marriage . . . it didn't seem a good solution. In fact, Jodie wasn't seeing much of Tim during those weeks.

Jodie and Tim realized a pregnancy was not enough reason for a long-time commitment.

Summer came, school was out, and she had told no one else. This simply couldn't happen to Jodie.

Then her best friend came to her for counseling. She and her boyfriend were very close and it was getting more and more difficult not to "go all the way." Did Jodie really think it would be a sin if they had sex? After all, they loved each other, and what harm would there be? What risks?

"I urged her not to . . . hinted at great risk. She didn't seem to hear me, didn't really think I knew what I was talking about," Jodie explained. "Finally I simply told her . . . told her I had been that route and that I was pregnant. She didn't believe me at first."

But this friend was her only confidant. Jodie was still president of the group at church. She continued her other activities there. Her long hot summer dragged by.

Should she go to the church retreat in the mountains in August? She would be at least five months pregnant by then. "I wished I could confide in my mother. But how could I hurt her?" she pondered. "I kept thinking, if she would only ask, simply say, 'Jodie, are you pregnant?' but she didn't."

Jodie went to the retreat and she found something there:

I found God as I never had before. I felt this terrific peace come over me. I suddenly realized my problems

would be worked out. I still had no idea how, but I
knew my life would somehow be OK.

She went home. The two girls who had gone to camp
with her had never realized she was pregnant. No one at
home seemed to have the slightest inkling. But finally her
mother said, "Jodie, I'm taking you to the doctor. We have
got to find out why you haven't had a period for so long."

"I was actually relieved," Jodie remembers. "Finally she
would know. But I still didn't tell her until I came out of
the doctor's office. Then I could finally say, 'Mom, I'm
pregnant.' I knew she'd help me."

Her mother's first reaction was, "Where did I go
wrong?" Her next, "What will you do?"

WHAT ABOUT MARRIAGE?

Tim came over. The family talked about various possi-
bilities. Was marriage the solution? Marriage would at least
help the situation as far as the church and, perhaps, their
own faith was concerned. But both Jodie and Tim realized
a pregnancy was not enough reason for a long-time
commitment. An aunt suggested marriage followed by a
quick annulment "so the baby would have a name." Jodie
couldn't see the value of "a name."

Jodie's senior year in high school would soon start. She
thought about her school and her friends there. She wasn't
about to join the yearly army of young girls who drop out
of school because of pregnancy. But neither did she want to
go back to her scheduled classes, to the counselor who had
taken such a special interest in her college plans, the physical education teacher who had been so proud of her out-
standing basketball record. She could go to Colorado, hide
at her aunt's home for the duration. She would have to . . .
want to . . . come back home some time.

Her sister told her of the special class for pregnant

students in her school district. She called the teacher the Friday before school started. The next day, a wet and dreary September Saturday (most September Saturdays in southern California are warm and bright . . . what happened today?) the teacher visited Jodie and her mother.

The teacher explained the special program, and pointed out that Jodie could continue her academic studies – her Civics, writing a research paper for Senior English. In addition, she could learn prepared childbirth techniques in the adaptive physical education class. (Childbirth takes as much conditioning and stamina as does starring in a basketball game, she was reminded.) She would have a chance to discuss the options available to herself and other pregnant teenagers.

Jodie and her mother implied that Jodie would keep the baby, that adoption was not an option they were considering at that time. "Although I certainly will back Jodie in whatever decision she makes," her mother assured the teacher.

Jodie enrolled in the school Monday. She got along well with the other girls, performed well academically, and found plenty of time (too much, according to her teacher) to talk with other students.

Two counselors from a youth counseling service volunteered each week to lead a rap session in the class. Emphasis was on learning to understand oneself and mention was seldom made of decision-making in regard to marriage versus single motherhood versus adoption. Jodie occasionally commented that she didn't know what she would do when the baby was born, but she didn't really want to talk to another counselor.

The teacher asked Jodie several times that fall if she would like to talk to Pat from the agency (and Pat asked the teacher lots of times) – but each time Jodie said, "No, not yet."

Pat, the on-call adoption agency counselor, was getting

nervous because she knew Jodie needed time to think
through her options. If she kept her baby, she would have a
lot of preparation to do before the baby was born. If she
decided to relinquish, she needed time to choose the "right"
family. And of course Tim would have to be involved in an
adoption decision

Finally, in early November, Jodie consented to see Pat.
They talked a number of times. As Jodie considered her
options, an adoption plan seemed the best course. After
more discussion, Tim also agreed to sign the adoption
papers.

The baby was due in early December.

Jodie had worked with her teacher to complete most of
her semester's course work by the time she delivered. They
agreed she might not want to come back to the special class
after delivery – without her baby. It could be difficult to
face all the others, each of whom was planning at that time
to keep her child.

By the first week in December, she was ready. Most of
her work was done. She still had her research paper to
write, but she had completed the preliminaries, and she

knew she could do that at home after delivery.

The week went by . . . and the next week dragged on
with nothing but a few false labor contractions. Pat was
leaving for the Christmas holidays so she gave Jodie another social worker's phone number. By the end of the third
week, Pat had flown back to Kansas City to be with her
family.

Jodie was feeling – and looking – very large, rather tired,
and eager for this whole thing to be over. Not that it would
ever be over, exactly – she knew this experience would be
in her memory forever, but . . . well, she was ready for it to
be in her memory, not her body!

School was out for the Christmas holidays on December
17. Saturday and Sunday seemed interminable as Jodie
tried to get into the spirit of preparing for Christmas with
her mother and little sister.

Sunday was especially hard. She hadn't gone to her
church since November. One of the women had told her
mother she didn't think Jodie should go to worship after
she "showed."

Jodie was hurt, and says now that she most needed her
church then. But she cared about other people's feelings
enough to go along with this viewpoint.

Monday . . . then Tuesday, and still no baby. Wednesday
morning the contractions started. The doctor said she would
have the baby by evening . . . but it was 24 hours before her
son was finally born – December 23, three weeks later than
expected.

It didn't occur to Jodie that day or the next to phone
Joyce, the social worker whose phone number Pat had
given her. She was too tired to think of much of anything.

A MEMORABLE CHRISTMAS

Saturday – Christmas morning – Jodie's doctor told her
she could go home if she liked, that Christmas Day was

reason enough for her to leave a day early.

But what about the baby? She suddenly realized nothing
had been finalized.

She frantically called Joyce . . . no answer. Jodie had had
Pat's home number for a month, but only Joyce's office
number. No one answered. (Adoption agency people
celebrate Christmas too.)

What could she do? She didn't want to spend Christmas
Day in the hospital.

The hospital would not keep the baby without the
mother. The only solution was to take the baby home
with her.

The house was full of relatives. Jodie was tired. She
hadn't been around infants much, and she hadn't been
involved in the baby care classes at school or in the hospital. She had ignored them because she wasn't keeping her
baby. But she managed that day with her mother's help.
She called Joyce the next day, but still no answer. Could it
be she wasn't "meant" to give up her baby? She was beginning to wonder.

Next morning her mother went off to work. A little later,
Jodie dialed Joyce's number again.

"This is Children's Home Society. To whom do you
wish to speak?"

"Joyce Smith, please."

"Just a minute. I'll ring her office."

"Hello, this is Joyce."

Two hours later Joyce picked up the baby. Jodie and Tim
signed the final papers a few days later, and the baby was
placed with the couple Jodie and Pat had selected.

Jodie went back to her high school for her last semester,
graduated with her class, and went on to college as she had
planned.

She also returned to her church soon after she had released her baby. A few months later she was asked to lead a
group of junior high girls. She became more and more

active in her church. Occasionally she shares with her junior high group and others her experiences with her baby.

When someone has a problem, the minister often says, "Go see Jodie . . ."

RONDA – PREGNANT AGAIN

Many teenagers who have had one child have another within one or two years. Girls who remain in school, however, have a much lower rate of repeat pregnancies. But it does happen.

Ronda dropped by school one rainy February afternoon with her announcement. John, 2, was with her.

I'm pregnant again . . . but I'm going to give it up for adoption.

"What about Dennis?"

We split two months ago – before I knew I was pregnant. When I called to tell him I was, he was very upset. I've already called Pat, and we have an appointment with her next week.

I had trouble taking the pill. I tried several kinds, and I was on it when I got pregnant this second time. In fact, I went to the doctor to renew my prescription, and after he examined me, he told me I was two months pregnant!

I haven't considered an abortion. I figure the baby has a right to live and I don't have a right to take that life. Somebody else who can't have kids should have him (or her). So I decided on adoption right away.

The nurses tried to talk me out of adoption.

---

*I took care of Seth while we were in the hospital –
fed him and diapered him. The nurses kept trying to
talk me out of adoption. They had been there when I
had John, so they were surprised that I was giving this
one up. They had their own opinions, but I didn't think
it was any of their business.*

*A friend of mine took a picture of Seth while he was
in the nursery. Of course I still have it.*

**"I think about Seth all the time,
but it doesn't bother me. I know it
was better for him, better for me,
and better for John."**

---

*I never met Seth's family. They're outdoor people –
like to camp and fish – and they're into athletics.
Dennis wanted our son to be able to camp, play ball,
and do all those things that Dennis enjoys so much.*

"What could you say to a 15-year-old who is pregnant,
something that might help her with her decisions?"

*Each person is different – I suppose I would tell her
to do what she thinks is best for her and her baby, not
what someone else thinks would be best for them. You
start feeling closed in sometimes. My mother offered
to help with John at first, but I just took him all to
myself. This made it hard when I first came home.*

*If there is someone to help, let them. My mom used
to tell me, "You go out and I'll take care of him," but I
wouldn't do it. I'd stay with him – and you know how
frustrated I got.*

*I think about Seth a lot, but it doesn't bother me. I
know it was better for him, better for me, better for
John. John takes all my time. If Seth has a family of
his own, he'll get that much more love and attention.*

ADOPTIVE PARENTS PAY COUNSELING FEES

Adoptive parents pay fees covering a portion of the cost of counseling services to them and to the birthparent(s) both before and after adoption. Fees are usually on a sliding scale based on the adoptive couple's income. The fee includes cost of services to the family and the child after the placement has been made.

An agency generally cannot provide financial assistance to the birthmother, but the social worker should be able to refer you to others who will give you the help you need.

If you do decide on adoption, the agency will take care of all the legal aspects. They stay abreast of new legislation and are very aware of your needs. They want whatever is best for you.

Doctors and lawyers often consider the adoptive family to be their primary client. If they do, they may not act in your best interest because they are thinking first of the adoptive family. You may decide to work with an agency for these reasons.

FOSTER CARE

Ronda mentioned that Seth had had *foster* care for a short period of time before he went to his adoptive parents' home. He didn't go to his permanent home until after his father had signed the adoption papers.

A foster family takes care of children on a short-term basis. The child's parents keep legal custody of him/her.

---

*Many children are placed in
foster care and left there for a
long time while their parents try
to "pull themselves together."*

Sometimes foster care is used by a mother who has not decided whether she wants to keep her baby or place him for adoption. She may request that the baby be placed in a foster home while she makes up her mind.

This can be a good approach if you know you haven't made a firm decision when the baby is born. Perhaps all you need are two or three weeks to think through your situation. You may realize, however, that if you take the baby home with you, you probably couldn't bear to give her up later – even if your head told you that would be best for both of you.

Although foster care is meant for short-term situations like this, it is often misused. Many children in the United States have been placed in foster care, left there for a long time, years in some cases, while their parents try to "pull themselves together." In the meantime, the child may be shifted from one foster home to another, never having the love and caring that a permanent family could give him. This is very hard on a child.

The child in foster care keeps his family's name. Foster parents are paid the cost of clothes, room, and board. If the placement is voluntary, the child's parent (or parents) may return at any time, or the child may be transferred to another foster home.

The foster mother, although she may be warm and caring, usually will not allow herself to love the child as if he were her own. This is because he could be – and often is – taken away after a short (or long) period of time.

Children need "real" parenting, whether from their birthparents or adoptive parents. Foster care can provide short-term help. For the sake of the child, however, it should never be considered a long-term solution to the possible problems of caring for your child yourself.

5

INDEPENDENT ADOPTION

Parents who relinquish to an adoption agency usually have some choice in the selection of the adoptive family for their baby. Many agencies allow, even encourage the birthparents to choose and meet the people who will become their child's adoptive parents.

In some parts of the United States and throughout Canada, however, licensed adoption agencies don't generally handle "open" adoptions. The birthparents and the adoptive parents don't meet and do not know each other's names and addresses. Birthparents who want to be more involved in planning their baby's adoption may decide on *independent* adoption, hoping to have more freedom in these matters.

Independent adoption means, by definition, an adoption in which the birthparents select the adoptive family. They place their child directly with that family. A few states do not allow independent placement of children, but most do.

---

*If birthparents decide to "go
independent," they should
consult a reputable lawyer.*

To make the placement legal, the birthparents sign a
"consent to adoption." This names the specific couple with
whom their child is placed. In nearly every state this consent must be signed in the presence of a representative of
the State Department of Social Services or its local
designee.

The lawyer can take consent from the birthparents to
place the child with the prospective adoptive family. This
is termed the "Take into care" form and is *not* the final
adoption paper.

If birthparents decide to "go independent," it is important
that they consult a reputable lawyer. When birthparents
relinquish to an agency, the agency takes care of all the
legal matters for them. In an independent adoption, birthparents are *on their own* – unless they choose to work with
an independent adoption service. Legal help is essential
whether the baby goes to relatives or to strangers.

In actual practice in independent adoption, the birthparents may not know the family which adopts their baby.
Sometimes a girl's doctor "knows someone." Or she may
go to a lawyer who specializes in adoption services. The
lawyer may have several, perhaps many, clients who wish
to adopt a baby. He may tell the young woman about one
or more families and suggest she make the choice.

---

*"He told us about independent
adoption and said he knew
someone who could help us."*

Usually a baby who is independently placed will go home from the hospital with its new family. In most states, the adoptive family is not studied to determine its fitness to adopt the child until *after the baby is already in their home.*

At that time, after they already have the child, the couple files an adoption petition in court. The state agency must study them to decide if they are fit to have this baby. Will they love him and provide a good family life for him? Is the child suitable for this particular family?

The state agency also interviews the birthparents to learn about family background, medical history, etc. This information is given to the adoptive family to share with their child.

ANNE MEETS ADOPTIVE PARENTS

Anne chose independent adoption. She's glad she did because in her case this meant meeting her baby's adoptive parents before delivery. Knowing they were "nice" people was reassuring.

Two weeks after her fourteenth birthday Anne suspected she was pregnant. She pushed the idea out of her mind, however, and did nothing about it for nearly five months. Her boyfriend finally insisted on taking her to the clinic for a pregnancy test:

I thought at the time I could get an abortion. The doctor didn't tell me what to do, didn't examine me. He just referred me to someone else. Next morning I decided I had to tell my mom because I couldn't do that (get an abortion) all by myself. So I got up, woke my mom, and told her. It was kind of sad.

She took me to our doctor that same day and he told us I was too far along – it would be illegal to get an abortion here in California. He said I could fly to New

*York and get one there but that would have had to be a
saline abortion and I didn't want that.*

*He asked if I was interested in adoption. He told us
about independent adoption and said he knew someone who could help us if that's what we wanted.
That's when I first started thinking about adoption.
Until that visit I assumed I would have an abortion.*

*I didn't go back to my regular school after that. My
mom knew about the special school for pregnant girls
and she called the teacher. The next week was spring
vacation so I had some time to think. I enrolled the
following Monday. By then my whole school knew
I was pregnant.*

"Did you get much flack at school?"

*No, I really didn't. By the time I enrolled in the
special school, I figured I would place the baby for
adoption. I guess my parents influenced my thinking,
but I agreed that adoption was the best thing. Of
course I thought about it a lot. I knew I didn't have to,
that being young doesn't stop a lot of people from
keeping the baby, but that wasn't what I wanted.*

**"My parents didn't push me
but they thought adoption
was a good idea."**

---

*The other pregnant girls would sometimes say,
"Well, I certainly would never give my baby up."
Most of them were against adoption, although I think
one or two were kind of leaning toward it. It didn't
bother me too much.*

*Of course I was sad that I wasn't going to have a
baby and everyone else in the class was. I still realized
what would happen and I knew what I wanted.*

The teacher sometimes showed films and held discussions about what really happens if you're in high school and are trying to take care of a baby too – or if you drop out of school. I knew I didn't want that!

"You always seemed very secure in your choice. Why do you suppose you made this decision?"

Perhaps the way I was raised. My parents didn't push me but they thought adoption was a good idea. A lot of the girls in the class wanted to get married (because of pregnancy), but I didn't even think of that.

After I decided I wanted to go through independent adoption, my parents called a lawyer. When I was about seven months pregnant, she (my lawyer) showed me the file on the couple who were to adopt my baby.

I read the whole thing – it told their histories, where they lived, what kind of work they did, etc. Then my lawyer gave them my phone number, and two or three weeks later they called to ask if they could come over to meet me. Of course we wanted them to. They came that Sunday.

My parents were here, and they all talked a lot. The couple was so nice, and they made me feel about one hundred times better about the whole thing. I knew then that my baby would have the kind of parents I wanted for him.

"If you give a baby up for adoption, you're making an accident into something really good. You're giving something wonderful to someone else."

HOSPITAL NURSE
IS SUPPORTIVE

I saw my baby when he was born, and before I left the hospital I visited him in the nursery. One nurse bothered me.

She told me, "Well, if it was up to me, I wouldn't let you see it." That made me mad because it was none of her business.

Another nurse, though, was especially nice. She talked to me a lot – told me that she had had a baby when she was 16. I appreciated her, because it's those first few hours and days that are the hardest when you give up your baby.

For the first two weeks after I had him I was really wondering about adoption. What it really comes down to is it doesn't matter how I felt – you have to think about the baby and how he'll have a better life with someone else.

"Do you think about him often?"

Well, yes, I think about him, but I don't worry about him. I've put it all behind me, but I certainly haven't forgotten about him.

"So much is being said and written now about 'open records' – the idea that some adoptees want very much to find their birthparents but often can't. Their birth records were sealed when they were adopted and can't be released on request in many states. Your baby's parents have met you, and your child can find you later if he likes. Does the idea bother you?"

Not at all. I have always thought in the back of my head that maybe I'll meet him sometime. Perhaps I'll go looking for him but I probably won't go up and tell him. They asked me when I signed the final papers if it would be all right if he looked for me. Of course I said that would be fine.

I can understand why some adoptive parents would worry that if there is no secrecy, the birthmother might come back and want the baby. But I think they would also like to see where their baby is coming from. My son's parents told me they were glad they'd met me.

"If a pregnant 14-year-old or an older woman unhappily pregnant asked you for advice, what would you tell her?"

I would say you have to think about it a lot before you make any kind of decision at all. You have to consider yourself and you have to consider the baby. You have to remember that the baby has to come before yourself.

The way I look at it is – if you give a baby up for adoption, you're making an accident that could be bad into something really good. You're giving something wonderful to someone else. I know I made those two people very happy. I know I don't have guilt feelings about that!

LAWYER'S ROLE

Anne mentioned "her" lawyer. She and her parents hired a lawyer to represent *them*. Her baby's adoptive parents were represented by a different lawyer. This is much better than having one lawyer represent both birth- and adoptive parents.

If one lawyer handles the entire case, a lawyer hired by the adoptive parents, she may not act in the best interests of the birthparents. If the birthmother, for example, considers changing her mind and keeping her child, the adoptive

parents' lawyer would tend to think first of the rights and
wishes of her primary clients, the adoptive parents. She
might even attempt to talk the young mother into releasing
her baby against her wishes.

In California, more infants are placed for adoption independently than through agencies, according to David
Leavitt. Leavitt is an attorney in Beverly Hills, California,
whose entire practice consists of handling independent
adoption cases.

"When couples come in telling me they want to adopt a
baby," Leavitt explained, "they fill out a rather complete
questionnaire first. Then I talk with them for at least two

hours. In that time I can spot dingalings – and if I do, I turn them away. Most people who want to adopt are pretty good people."

"How do you decide who gets which baby?" I asked.

"Many of my clients find their own babies," he answered. "During that first interview I tell them how to go about finding an adoptable infant. I suggest they make out a resume complete with their picture, reasons they want to adopt, their income, profession, where they live, hobbies, and other details about their lives.

"Obstetricians are the best sources for information about an adoptable baby. So I advise them to get that resume to as many obstetricians as possible. Many of them come back later with information about a baby who, when born, will be available for adoption."

Because state law in California declares that the independent adoption is a placement by the birthparents to the adoptive parents, strict interpretation of the law would allow the lawyer *only* to perform necessary legal services for the baby's two sets of parents. Those who follow this interpretation believe he should not "match" babies and adoptive families.

In actual practice, however, couples who want to adopt a child frequently ask a lawyer or obstetrician, sometimes their minister, rabbi, or priest, if they know of "available" children. A young woman who is unhappily pregnant may ask her doctor what she can do. Or her doctor may ask her if she is interested in placing for adoption.

When a prospective birthmother approaches Leavitt, he talks to her, learns something about her and her wishes for her child. He then chooses from among his clients a family he thinks would be appropriate. He hands the young woman a file containing information about the couple. Usually a photograph is included. Almost always, he says, she agrees to the first family he picks.

Leavitt likes to speak of an adoption as a marriage

between the baby and its adoptive parents. "I treat the young birthmother as the father of the bride," he said. "If I do my job properly, she will know all about that family and she will feel good about them parenting her baby."

BIRTHPARENTS MEET ADOPTIVE PARENTS

After the selection is made (but before the baby is born), the adoptive parents are called. They then telephone the birthmother to ask if they can meet her. Usually they meet at a restaurant for dessert. Often both the adoptive parents and the birthmother are reassured by this meeting.

When the baby is born, the adoptive parents generally send flowers to its mother, Leavitt said. "After all, she's the mother of their baby and they love her," he commented.

Leavitt's last contact with the young woman is usually in the hospital the day after she delivers her baby. The adoptive parents take the baby home from the hospital. Consent to adoption, as stated above, is not signed until the state agency has checked out the family.

The birthmother can never give her consent to adopt directly to the adoptive parents, to the doctor, or to the lawyer. She must give that consent to the social worker who represents the state.

Before she signs that consent, the social worker will tell her about the adoptive parents. If she doesn't like what she hears, she can request that her baby be returned to her. At that time she can still relinquish to an adoption agency if she wishes, although this seldom happens.

COSTS OF ADOPTION

If you make an independent adoption plan for your baby, the adoptive parents you choose are expected to pay the legal and other costs of the adoption.

However, it is absolutely illegal for prospective adoptive parents to give the birthmother money as a gift. Whatever she receives to pay medical bills and possibly her living expenses during pregnancy must be reported to the court. If you are ever approached by someone who wants to pay you to let them adopt your child, you should report that person to the authorities immediately!

It is lawful for the adoptive parents to pay for prenatal care and hospital stay. In some cases, they may contribute toward essential living expenses during the latter part of pregnancy.

They must file a statement when they adopt that they have paid only pregnancy costs and lawyer/agency fees. The law has always permitted this. If something more is added, it's illegal.

A criticism sometimes leveled at independent adoption is that, because the adoptive parents pay at least the birthmother's medical bills, she would have trouble changing her mind about the adoption. Even though she doesn't sign the consent to adopt until about six weeks after delivery, she might find it difficult to back out of such an arrangement.

However, the birthmother has no legal obligation to pay back the expense money she received from the prospective adoptive family. According to law, she cannot release her child for adoption until after delivery. Money spent before delivery by the adoptive parents is spent in the hope and expectation of adopting that baby, but it is not dependent on the adoption being finalized.

The adoptive parents and/or their lawyer cannot legally say, "If you decide to keep your baby, you must pay back the money spent on your medical and other pregnancy bills." Sometimes, if a young woman decides to keep her baby, her parents will choose to repay the money spent on her pregnancy needs. They will not be required by law to do so, however.

EXPERIENCED LAWYER
IS PREFERABLE

Research from several years ago (1978: *Adoptions Without Agencies: A Study of Independent Adoption)* suggests that most attorneys who handle adoption cases do so only occasionally. The study reported that lawyers with larger adoption practices tended to discuss alternatives and refer to agencies more often than did those who handled only an occasional adoption. The lawyers who placed babies more often also tended to collect more background information on the birthparents. This may mean less risk to the birthmother and the adoptive parents who "go independent" if they work with a lawyer with more experience in adoption cases.

An unskilled lawyer may cause problems in independent adoption. A student who released her child at birth thought the adoption was final. Six weeks later she learned she must fly across the country (at the adoptive parents' expense) to sign the final papers. She felt tricked.

One young woman I interviewed had been told by her doctor that her baby's adoptive father was a lawyer. She had also assumed the mother would stay home to care for her infant.

It wasn't until after the home study had been done that she learned the father was really a free-lance photographer employed only part-time. She also learned the mother was a nurse working in the hospital where the baby had been delivered.

She felt cheated. But she didn't consider taking her child back. He had been with his adoptive parents two months and it didn't make sense to his birthmother to take him from the parents he had already learned to love. She was simply frustrated at being deceived.

Her frustration could, perhaps, have been prevented if she had asked more questions in the beginning.

If you release a child for independent adoption, you know there is no agency doing a thorough check on your baby's future family. You have not only a right, but also a responsibility to be as sure as you can possibly be that the couple receiving your baby are the kind of people *you* want to parent your child.

Anne was delighted to meet her baby's adoptive parents. With independent adoption, even if the two sets of parents don't meet, the names of each are on the consent-to-adoption paper. This, of course, means secrecy is not part of the arrangement.

WENDI SUE CHOOSES BABY'S PARENTS

When Wendi Sue's parents urged her to consider adoption, she saw an adoption lawyer first. She was turned off by this particular attorney because his goal seemed to be to find the richest adoptive parents possible for Wendi Sue's baby. She knew that wasn't all she wanted for her child.

Her teacher suggested an independent adoption service in the next town. Wendi Sue shares her story:

After I missed two periods, I told my mom. She took me to the doctor the next day and he said I was eight weeks pregnant. I started crying and then my mom started crying.

A week later we began talking about adoption. At first she and my dad said I could keep the baby, but if I did, I couldn't live at home. Four months later they said I could stay at home with the baby until I finished school. By then I had made up my mind on adoption.

After talking with that lawyer, I decided I wanted more help than he could give by himself. I didn't think I wanted to work with an agency so I went to an independent adoption service. First the counselor and

I talked a long time about my decision. She said adoption shouldn't be decided quickly.

She showed me a lot of files. They were from people who wanted to adopt a baby. Each one included pictures and a lot of information about the family. I went through a stack of them, then decided on Betty and Carl.

I called them and said, "I'm Wendi Sue, and I wonder if you guys would like to adopt my baby." Betty screamed so loud I couldn't hear for several hours. That same day they came over here to my house and we talked.

I saw them several times before Mandy was born. Betty took me shopping and we went to a show. We talked about normal things. She showed me the baby's room, and it was so cute.

I said I didn't want to see my baby, but after she was born, I changed my mind completely. Betty and Carl came to see me after Mandy was born. They were there with my mom and dad and my brother.

My mom asked Betty if she wanted to hold the baby first, and she said, "No, she's your first grandchild and you should hold her." Of course I had already held Mandy.

The next morning I was feeding the baby when Betty and Carl walked in. They took one look at me and started crying. Betty came over and gave me a big hug and they both thanked me over and over.

Suddenly, as Wendi Sue was talking, she jumped up and went into her bedroom. She came back carrying a photo album and showed me dozens of pictures of Mandy. Also in the album was a letter from Betty to Wendi Sue: "Thank you for a miracle of love and a chance at being a mother. God bless you always and know in your heart that you are worthy of the love of others, especially ours."

Latest additions to the album were pictures of two-month-old Mandy in the outfit Wendi Sue had given her for Easter. The album contained letters, cards, valentines, adoption papers, and pictures of Wendi Sue before she delivered. There were also lots of pictures taken in the hospital including a beautiful photo of Wendi Sue showing the adoptive parents how to swaddle their baby.

They always welcomed me when I went to see them. I would call a week ahead and ask if I could come visit. I've been there several times.

Now that I've signed the papers, I don't plan to see them much, if at all. They said I'm welcome, but I think we each need to get on with our lives.

I think other girls should consider adoption. They shouldn't keep the baby because they feel they have to. If they give the baby up for adoption, they can know they are not being selfish, that they are doing something right.

I signed the papers a week ago. I felt real hurt, but not angry hurt. I was glad it was over but it was just sad to see her go. I did it because it felt right to me, but I was still sad.

Some adoptive parents would find it difficult to accept as much interaction with their baby's birthmother as Wendi Sue describes. However, many people feel the birthparents are *less* likely to want their child back if they have met the adoptive family. Through meeting their child's new family, the birthparents can be satisfied that their child is receiving the love and caring they want for him/her.

James Edson, attorney in Long Beach, California, provides legal services for about 30 adoptions each year. While his clients are the adoptive parents, the majority of the birthparents involved are working with an independent adoption service in his area.

When asked about contact between the birth- and adoptive parents, Edson commented, "She doesn't necessarily meet the adoptive parents, but if she wants to, she can. We work out special arrangements.

"She may want pictures every year, see the baby once in awhile. Some adoptive parent clients are open and friendly and are willing to let the child know his birthmother."

LACK OF COUNSELING MAY BE A PROBLEM

You might choose independent adoption because you want to meet your baby's future parents. You may also want to know your baby will go home with them directly from the hospital. You need to realize the risks in the lack of counseling for you and in the lack of a home study of the adoptive parents *before* they receive your child.

The biggest criticism of independent adoption is the lack of counseling usually available. Leavitt, for example, assumes his clients know that they want to release for adoption when they come into his office. He offers no counseling service.

This lack of counseling can be a serious risk in independent adoption. In some areas, however, independent adoption services are available. With a good adoption service, birthparent clients may receive the same high-quality counseling they might expect from a licensed adoption agency.

If you do consider independent adoption, *be sure* to contact a reputable lawyer for advice. If you adopt through an agency, they will handle the legal matters. *But in independent adoption, it's up to you.*

6

SOMETIMES RELATIVES ADOPT

Some young mothers – about 2.5 percent of all pregnant teenagers – place their babies with relatives or friends who then raise the child. If this placement is legalized as an adoption, it is considered one kind of independent adoption.

During her pregnancy Rosa came to southern California from Tennessee to live with her older cousin and his wife. Her friends in Tennessee never knew she was pregnant. Her cousin and his wife already had three preschoolers but, when they first learned she was pregnant, agreed to adopt her baby.

Luckily for her plans, her baby was due in August. She managed to conceal the fact of her pregnancy until school was out. She flew immediately to California where she stayed until two weeks after her baby was born. She then flew home and enrolled in her junior year of high school.

Rosa seems satisfied with the situation. She doesn't have

the responsibility of parenting her child, but she knows
where he is and how he's getting along.

POSSIBLE PROBLEMS
IN RELATIVE ADOPTION

For some birthparents, this can be a bad decision. Seeing
her baby reared by someone else can be hard on the
birthmother even if, perhaps because she is close to that
person. She may decide three or four years later that she
should be raising her "own" child. If so, she will probably
find that her baby's adoptive parents, although related to
her, aren't willing to give up the child they consider
their own.

One young woman who sent her baby to live with her
sister in another state said, "When Jennie is old enough to
understand, I'll ask her if she would rather live with me or
with my sister." This would probably be unfair to the child
as well as to the adoptive (or foster) parents.

A child who lives with one set of parents for several
years – or even one year – usually considers those parents
to be the "real" parents. Being asked to choose between
them and someone else who considers herself his "real"
mother can be devastating. Sometimes, however, relative
adoption works beautifully:

LYNN'S STORY

Lynn called me at school one chilly November day. "Will
you tell me about your class?" she asked.

Two hours later I was talking with her and her mother in
their comfortable, upper-middleclass home. Her mother
was busily preparing a turkey for roasting. She explained
they were taking it with them the next evening on a
Thanksgiving weekend camping trip. Several brothers and
sisters walked in and out as we talked.

"We haven't decided for sure,
but we probably will place
the baby for adoption."

Lynn's father appeared briefly. He had recently started a printing business which kept him very busy.

"Lynn will stay with us during her pregnancy," her mother said. "We haven't decided for sure, but we think we'll probably place the baby for adoption. Lynn isn't ready to be a parent."

She excused herself to answer the telephone and I glanced at petite, pretty, 15-year-old Lynn. Her eyes were filling with tears. It appeared that "we" weren't sold on the idea of an adoption plan for the coming baby.

So often a teenager hides the fact of her pregnancy from her family – even from herself, it seems. Lynn was different. Just a few weeks earlier she had been hospitalized because of a bronchial condition. Her doctor came into her room for a final check before releasing her to go home. He had an amazing announcement. She was five weeks pregnant.

Lynn discussed her predicament:

An hour later Ron – the baby's father – came in and I told him. He said we could cope with it. Soon my mother arrived, and we told her together. She was, of course, upset, and most of all, hurt. She went home and told my Dad. I was discharged from the hospital late that afternoon.

And would you believe that all three of my out-of-state sisters called me that night – for no special reason – and we told them. My grandmother also called. It was weird how fast they all knew about it that same night.

*There were so many options open because I was
only five weeks pregnant. Abortion would be the first
thing to think about if you didn't want a baby, but I
couldn't do that. We talked and talked. Ron came over
on Sunday and we talked with my parents for a long
time. We finally decided I would live at home during
the pregnancy. Then if we still loved each other, we
would get married after the baby was born.*

LYNN DECIDES TO ENROLL IN TEEN MOTHER PROGRAM

Lynn continued going to school each day, but a few
weeks later she made the phone call to the special class for
pregnant students. She enrolled in the class the Monday
following our visit.

A few days before Christmas vacation I brought up the
subject of adoption. Once more the tears started, and I
realized the time wasn't right. "We haven't decided," was
all she said.

A couple of months later Lynn told me her decision. She
had decided to let her sister, who lives several hundred
miles away, care for the baby "until I grow up."

The decision was the result of a phone call her mother
had made to her grandmother. She mentioned that Lynn
might place the baby for adoption.This was related to the
married sister who then called her mother. She urged them
to let her have the baby.

"Before the baby goes out of the family, I want to care
for it. Don't place it with strangers," she pleaded.

By this time Lynn had decided not to see Ron. As she
describes him, "He thinks he's the big man. He drinks a
little booze, then decides he can rule the world. He even
dated someone else. I felt if I couldn't depend on him now
when I need him most, how could I ever depend on him?"

Lynn seemed satisfied with the decision to place the baby with her sister for the time being. She was a tenth grader, but realized she could skip a year, earning her high school diploma a year later. She planned then to move in with her sister and baby, and attend the nearby university.

LYNN'S SISTER WILL PARENT

Lynn's baby was born. Her mother coached her during labor and delivery, and the three of them came back to class a few days later to share the experience. Then, a week after his birth, Brad went home with Diana, Lynn's sister.

Lynn remembers:

The hardest thing I have ever done in my entire life was to hand Brad to Diana as she got on that airplane. I had cared for him a week, and it was rough sending him away. I don't think I could have done it if I hadn't known I would soon see him again.

"If I had thought Brad would be better off with me, I would have taken him."

I went to see him about a month later. It was terribly hard leaving him again. But each time I visited him, and I did at least once a month that first year, it got a little easier. As time passed, I realized I simply wasn't ready to take care of a baby. And I didn't want to pawn him off on my mom and dad.

So I finally came to my senses and decided the only way I could cope with it and be the person I wanted to be was to let my sister adopt him. I signed the papers when he was almost two years old, and I haven't regretted one bit of it. I see him every once in awhile.

When she was 18, Lynn got her own apartment and a secretarial job she enjoyed. When asked if she felt she had missed something by skipping that year of high school, she replied:

> *No way. In fact, I can't imagine myself in high school this year. Maybe it would be fun going back, but I love where I am now. College maybe. I think I'll take a class or two this summer, and perhaps get into college this fall.*
>
> *When Brad was born, though, no one could have told me I would adopt that baby out. I would never have believed them. And I don't regret that I didn't do it sooner. If I had when he was born, I don't know how I would have felt. In those two years I realized there was no way I could take care of him the way I wanted him taken care of. By then he was, of course, walking and talking a lot.*
>
> *It was a hard decision. If I had thought Brad would have been better off with me, I would have taken him. But no way. He is in the best home I can imagine. He is so loved in that family. I couldn't see ruining a good thing.*
>
> *So many people say they have never seen a family adoption work, but he's three years old and there simply is no problem.*
>
> *I guess it's a lot because of the way I feel. I feel when I'm ready to have my family, I'll start it. I don't want to have my family too early when I can't deal with it.*

"Did the girls in the class influence you?"

> *No, I don't think so. It did bother me when they said, "How could you do that?" I thought to myself, "How could they do that to their babies?" I didn't*

mean it in spite. It just seemed too hard, not only for them, but for their babies.

"It's not like playing house. It's the real thing."

I think I'm a lot happier person now without having a child, and I think Brad is happier where he is. I don't see how girls who are 14, 15, even 16, can have a baby, perhaps get married. How can they deal with it? I think if I had gone that route, I would be divorced now and would have had a sad life these past two years.

Lynn still sees Brad fairly often. A few months before she and Mike were married, Mike took her up to see Brad. Brad and his family often spend holidays with Lynn and her parents.

When I go up there he feels just like another nephew. It isn't that I don't love him. I would do anything for him today, but I don't feel like I'm a mother now . . . and I'm not. I really never was except for that one week.

Perhaps I shouldn't say this because it may make me sound uncaring, but it wasn't hard for me to sign those adoption papers. Not nearly as hard as putting him on that plane when he was one week old.

Of course it wasn't an easy breezy thing. I was nervous, but it wasn't terribly difficult because I had made my decision a month or two before. I didn't tell anybody for awhile because I wanted to make sure. I really thought through whether or not I would regret doing this, and I decided I would not.

It would have been much harder to sign those papers when he was first born. I'm happy my sister

was willing to take him home then without waiting for
the final adoption decision.

DEAR ABBY'S
ADVICE HELPS

Soon after I learned I was pregnant and was still
attending my old school, I worked for a teacher in the
activities office. She and I were alone one day, talking.
I had told her I was pregnant, and she brought me a
little newspaper clipping. I think that little article
influenced me as much as anything. I think I still have
it . . . yes . . . here it is.

"Dear Abby,
  "I am 16 and eight months pregnant. I made an
important decision a few weeks ago. I decided to give
my baby up for adoption. Abby, I love this baby very,
very much. That is why I'm giving it up. Some people
say I am cruel and even selfish, but I think it would be
much more selfish to keep the baby and make it suffer
for my mistakes.
  "I have always respected your opinion, Abby. Do
you think I made the right choice?
                            Expecting the Best in Texas"

"Dear Expecting. Yes. God bless you."

I think this had a big effect on me. You have to
consider what's best for your baby. It's not like play-
ing house. It's not like dressing him up and showing
him off – it's the real thing. You have to realize your
baby must have the best. It's not only you that matters.
  When I was pregnant, I thought, "How can I do
this, how can I adopt my baby out?" I know now it
was the best thing for the baby and for me.

Four years after Brad was born, Lynn and Mike were married. They had a lovely church wedding, and Brad was their handsome little ringbearer.

VERA TRIES PARENTING

Vera never considered adoption while she was pregnant. She "knew" she would keep her baby and raise it herself. While she was pleasant to the two girls who were making an adoption plan that semester, she had commented to me, "How could anyone give up her baby?"

She discovered that caring for a baby full-time was harder than she had expected. She began to wonder, much as she loved Grant, if perhaps the baby would be better off with someone more ready to settle down to the constant care he demanded:

I never thought I would let anybody else take care of him, but it happened. I wasn't able to give him all the things he needed, and besides, I really didn't know how to take care of him.

---
*"When he was six months old,
I decided I couldn't handle it."*

Grant's father and I met when I was 14. We were going to get married as soon as I turned 16, but the first time I saw him hold Grant, I thought, "He can't do that." I couldn't realize the baby was his too. From that minute I knew we would break up. So one day I said, "You know, I'm not going to marry you," and he left.

Being pregnant was so neat. I remember when the baby would kick me and the funny feelings I'd get in my stomach – it felt like butterflies. Sometimes when I was lying on the couch, he would turn completely

*around. Once a friend brought a stethoscope over, and
I could feel his heartbeat. It was weird.*

*After Grant was born it was hard getting up in the
middle of the night every single night. Every time he
cried I picked him up, and I had trouble taking care of
him without falling asleep myself. Then he'd wake up
again early in the morning, and in the afternoon when
I wanted to take a nap. God, I was tired!*

*You have to clean him, change his diapers, clean up
his room so it won't smell, wash his clothes, mix his
formula just right. First you have to find the right one
or he'll be sick. He had a lot of problems with his formula. I took him to another doctor who said he was
getting too much solid food. He put Grant on plain
cereal and not much of that. He was about two months
old then, and he started feeling better.*

VERA MAKES
A DECISION

*When he was six months old I decided I couldn't
handle it. I asked my sister-in-law to take him, but she
wouldn't. She already had a baby two months younger
than Grant.*

*I tried a little longer, but if you go to school, you
don't have time to take care of a baby. He was beginning to think my mother was his real mom. I didn't
think that was good. He'd be confused at having
two moms.*

*We called my sister in Arizona. She already has
two kids and she said she'd be glad to take Grant. She
hasn't adopted him – she's just his legal guardian.*

*Marge (my sister) couldn't come get him for almost
a month, so my mom took over. Sometimes people
criticized me because I wasn't taking care of him
myself, but I felt I was missing out on things with my*

*friends and I didn't want that any longer. I feel kind of
bad about that now. I should have taken care of him
until he left. Now I miss him and want to go see him.*

*What hurt me the most was the day he left. He had
just learned to crawl and I wanted to sit and watch
him crawl forever!*

"Didn't you talk to an adoption agency counselor?"

*Yes, once, but I couldn't stand the thought of never
seeing Grant again. I feel better knowing where he is
and that I can keep in touch with him. When he's old
enough to understand, I'll probably ask him if he
would like to come back to live with me. If he says no,
I'll understand.*

*I want him to know I gave him to my sister because
I love him, because I wanted him to have the things
and the care he needed. I think I did the right thing.
Some people don't understand, but I know why I did it.
As long as I know, that's what counts.*

"How would your sister feel if you took him back?"

*She'd be hurt, I know. She'd probably feel like I did
when Grant left. When I heard that car drive away
and I knew he was gone, I went in my bedroom and
cried and cried. I had to think — what would I have
done if I had kept him with no money? I couldn't have
handled it.*

"Any advice for other 14- or 15-year-olds?"

*Talk it over with someone you don't even know,
perhaps a total stranger. Make it clear you just want to
know how somebody else feels. You'll have to make
your own decision.*

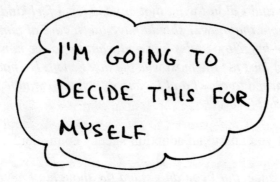

Then don't make that mistake again! Don't be
fooled by anybody saying he loves you. At 14, 15, even
16 – that's too young to understand motherhood, too
young to take care of a baby. You still want your
mother to take care of you at the same time you have to
care for your baby.

There are too many things to do – going to school,
taking care of the baby, just too many things pushed at
you if you get pregnant.

You can't live out the rest of your childhood – you
have to be a woman already. You'll never have the
experience of being a teenager. I just wish I had
thought first.

ADOPTIVE MOTHER EXPLAINS

Vince's mother also thought she could handle being a
teenage parent. In fact, Vince was her second baby, but her
life became harder and harder. Her babies' father never
helped support his children and welfare didn't stretch far
enough. Life was a drag. Vince's adoptive mother, Maria.
tells his story:

Vince was six months old when we took him. This
was a sudden thing. Teresa is my husband's sister,
and we knew she had a lot of problems. One day she

*called the family together because she didn't see how
she could care for her kids any longer.*

*She had two, Elisa who was three, and Vince.
Teresa was 18 then, and welfare was on her back.
They kept threatening to take both children away from
her. She knew by then she couldn't handle it, being a
mother, but she wanted the kids to stay in the family.*

"I know she decided to let us adopt him because she loved him."

---

*She said she wanted each of her brothers to take
one. Elisa went with Jose up north and they adopted
her. That's been a problem because Teresa lives in the
same town. She visits Jose's family often and brings
presents just for Elisa. She ignores their other kids
and that makes it hard for all of them.*

*We got away from that kind of pressure. We live
about 200 miles away from the rest of them.*

*When we went through legal adoption, it got com-
plicated. First, Teresa called us several times and said
she might change her mind. Then she said she really
couldn't keep him. Later his father turned up and said
flatly he wouldn't release him to us. So we had to go
through court and prove abandonment. We could do
this because he had never provided any support at all
for Vince.*

*Once we got to court, there was no problem. It's
official now. We still don't visit the family much
because I think it's hard for Teresa. They tell us she's
getting her life back together now.*

*I thought at first we would just baby-sit for awhile. I
was pretty insecure about the whole thing until I heard
that judge say, "This is your son." How we celebrated
that night!*

When we first got him, I got the after-baby blues

which really surprised me. He cried a lot the first
couple of days – I guess we all did. Now, of course,
I'm glad it happened. I had never understood before
why anybody would give up their child. Now I have a
great deal of respect for Teresa that she didn't fight
for him when it came down to the line at court. I know
it was hard for her. I know she decided to let us adopt
him because she knew she couldn't take care of him
and because she loved him.

She called us a month ago about a family matter. I
called Vince and asked him if he wanted to speak to
Teresa. He's three now, and of course he knows that
we adopted him. "You remember Teresa, don't you?"
I asked him.

He thought a minute, then said, "Oh, yes, she used
to be my mommy, didn't she?" and he trotted off to
talk to her on the phone.

I think it's worked out well for all of us.

MINORITY ADOPTION

Because family ties are especially strong in the Mexican
American culture, adoption occurs less frequently than it
does in Anglo and Black families. When it does occur,
family adoption, as in Vince's case, is more likely to
happen than is agency adoption. Someone in the extended
family will often help the birthmother/father when parenting becomes too hard.

However, Los Angeles adoption agency social workers
report a significant number of minority adoptions. An
Hispanic social worker commented that when he speaks to
classes of pregnant teenagers, he passes his card out indi-
vidually to the girls rather than to the teacher. "Sometimes
they just want to talk," he commented, "and if there were
less peer group or parental pressure they might choose to
release for adoption."

At one time few adoptive homes were available in Black or Hispanic communities. However, this situation has changed. "We don't have healthy Black or Hispanic babies waiting for placement," reported Janice Wills, Los Angeles County child welfare worker.

"We have plenty of homes available for Hispanic babies. In fact, we're now studying Hispanic families who registered one and two years ago. There simply aren't enough babies free for adoption by those who wish to adopt."

Ms. Wills also stated that in the past it was assumed that middle-class white girls placed their babies for adoption while Black teenagers always kept their infants. "I think this has changed," she said. "Now there is no big difference between whether the Black girl or Anglo girl keeps. This is certainly true with my clients."

SPECIAL ADOPTION LAW FOR NATIVE AMERICANS

Adoption plans for Native American children must follow different rules. "Before we can place an American Indian child for adoption, we must see if that child is registered with his/her tribe. If so, the tribe has priority for the placement of that child," Ms. Wills reported.

"If the tribe is not contacted, they can come back at any time and take the child away from the adoptive parents," she continued.

If your child is of Native American descent and you are considering an adoption plan, it is important that you find out about these special laws. If you're planning an independent adoption, be sure the attorneys are carefully following the regulations.

For more information, contact the Social Services of the tribal center or the American Indian Urban Center, Ms. Wills advised.

COMMON CRITICISM
OF RELATIVE ADOPTION

A criticism often leveled at family adoption is that the child may be "claimed" by both his birth- and adoptive parents. If the birthmother lives near or with her child, it can be frustrating and painful to see someone else bring up her son or daughter.

She may disagree strongly with the way "her" child is being reared. If she does, should she interfere? Or should she ignore the situation, knowing the child is no longer truly hers?

Judging from the stories of relative adoption told in this chapter, the best approach is truly to release to that relative the *full* responsibility for the child. Sharing the parenting role, while difficult for the parents, can be especially damaging to the child. Every child needs the security of knowing *one* set of parents is truly his.

For many young parents, watching their baby reared by someone else may be too difficult. Releasing their child to strangers – a couple carefully selected by themselves or their agency – may be a better approach for themselves and for their baby.

Vera mentioned she didn't consider agency adoption because she "couldn't stand the thought of never seeing Grant again." As mentioned before, birthparents today may be able to work with an agency which permits open adoption.

Some birth- and adoptive parents agree to a plan whereby the adoptive parents stay in contact with their child. In these situations, the child may be fully aware his birthparents gave him life while his adoptive parents are his "real" day-to-day parents.

Agency – independent – relative – three kinds of adoption, and each is legal in most states. Each method has its good points and its not-so-good aspects. Only you can decide which, if any, is best for you and for your baby.

7

BIRTHFATHERS HAVE RIGHTS

What rights should fathers have in adoption planning? What rights *do* fathers have?

Married couples, of course, normally share parental rights. If a married woman wishes to release her baby for adoption, her husband must also sign the legal relinquishment – even if he is not the child's father.

Years ago, an unmarried father's permission was not required if the mother wished to release the baby for adoption. Only the mother's signature was needed. Today, however, the father's signature, if he can be found, is almost always required before the adoption can be finalized.

If you are considering an adoption plan, it is extremely important that you know the law in your state or province regarding the father's signature in an adoption. Courts and agencies in most states insist that both parents must consent to the release of their child. In some states, the father, if he is known, must simply be notified that the birthmother is releasing their child for adoption.

If the father can't be found, agencies usually try to locate him. If they can't find him the court is petitioned to remove the rights of the absent or unknown father. After a certain period of time, the child can then be released for adoption.

CALIFORNIA LAW

The Uniform Parentage Act is a California law which became effective in 1976. A major aim of this Act is to erase the former distinction in status between legitimate and illegitimate children.

This was accomplished, but the Act sometimes presents a confusing situation to counselors and attorneys dealing with adoption of children whose parents are not married to each other.

Does the unmarried father, for instance, have a right to insist his baby's mother must raise that baby herself (without his help) even if she feels adoption is the best decision?

Stacey, after a great deal of painful soul searching, finally decided adoption was the best option for her baby. She had another year of high school, and she had always wanted to be a teacher. She knew she wanted to go to college and, although she wanted a family some day, this wasn't the right time.

If the mother doesn't wish to keep the child, the father has the right to custody.

But what about Curt? He, of course, also had to sign to release the baby. He and Stacey weren't seeing each other then, but Pat, the adoption agency social worker, pointed out that he had to be involved too. In the meantime, Curt had been discussing his situation with a young minister. Curt decided to bring the minister along for the conference with Stacey and Pat.

They met, first together, then Curt and Pat talked while Stacey and the young pastor discussed the situation. The pastor told Stacey he didn't think Curt should keep the baby. Neither should he marry Stacey because he was too immature for either marriage or parenthood.

However, the pastor admonished Stacey, she must not relinquish – she must keep the baby "because in the Bible no unmarried mother gives her baby up for adoption"!

Later that day Stacey discussed the situation with her pastor. He reminded her of Moses. "Now there was an adoptee who really made good," he commented wryly.

Curt finally agreed to sign relinquishment papers. The adoption proceeded smoothly from that point only because he did so.

TWO "KINDS" OF FATHERS

Sometimes a birthmother doesn't want her baby's father even to know she's pregnant. Or she may feel he'd be opposed to the adoption plan. She doesn't want him notified.

However, a birthfather may be as concerned about his baby's life as is the birthmother. Shutting the father out of the adoption planning can backfire.

If you're in this situation, you need to know the father's legal rights. You don't want the adoption stopped at some later time because he comes back to demand his rights as the child's other parent. You don't want your child's life disrupted after s/he is living with the adoptive family.

If you don't want to talk with him, perhaps you can help your adoption counselor make an appointment with him.

When he realizes the ultimate goal of an adoption plan is to provide a good life for his child, and that he may be part of that planning, he may decide to cooperate fully by signing the relinquishment papers.

The California Uniform Parentage law describes two kinds of fathers, "presumed" and "alleged." A man who has lived with the mother, is married to her when the child is born, or was married to her 300 days or less before the birth is usually considered the "presumed" father. If the mother doesn't wish to keep the child, he has the right to custody. Before that child can be placed for adoption, both parents must sign relinquishment – or court action must terminate parental rights.

Of course a joint relinquishment decision is preferable for all those concerned with the adoption.

SHOULD DENNIS KEEP HIS BABY?

When Ronda decided she couldn't give her baby the kind of life she wanted for him, she told her former boyfriend. Both of them then discussed the situation with Pat.

Dennis seriously considered keeping the baby. Ronda, though she would have preferred not to know where her baby was, didn't oppose. Dennis' plans. She knew she wasn't ready to care for the baby, but if Dennis' mother wanted to help him, more power to them. She had always thought very highly of Mrs. Aguerre.

Dennis and the social worker discussed the pros and cons of keeping versus making an adoption plan.

Dennis decided that even though his mother was willing to do so, she shouldn't quit her job because of his child. Since he was still in school, he knew he would have to have a great deal of her help if he became an "acting" father.

Dennis and Ronda decided together to place their child with another family. Both seem satisfied with the decision.

Ronda and Dennis, although never married, had lived together briefly early in her pregnancy. A "presumed" father may be established, however, even if the person in question has neither lived with nor been married to the mother. California Civil Code 7004 (a) (4) states a man may be presumed to be the father if "he receives the child into his home and openly holds out the child as his natural child."

In addition, a man who doesn't meet these liberal requirements as the presumed father may be considered the "alleged" father.

This happens if he is named as the father but does not meet the above requirements. The law still protects his rights in California by requiring his relinquishment, waiver of notice, or denial of paternity before a child relinquished by its mother can be placed.

In other words, the mother may name as the father on the birth certificate a man who meets none of the above "presumed" father requirements. If she does, her child cannot be released for adoption until the man named either denies he is the father, waives (gives up) in writing his rights to notice of the adoption hearing, or signs relinquishment for adoption.

The father who does not make a decision creates a difficult situation for the mother.

MARIO'S DECISION

Mario had said he might sign a paper denying he was the baby's father or he might sign for the relinquishment. He hadn't decided which he would do when the baby was born.

After his son's birth, he went to the hospital. First he stopped to see Sue. He said he wanted to see the baby. Sue, however, told him he couldn't see the infant unless he signed the relinquishment papers as the child's father.

"The baby has two parents. The rights of both must be terminated"

She knew he was the father. He knew it. He was listed on the birth certificate as the baby's father. If he chose to say at that point he was not, she was resigned to it. But she was firm in saying he had no right to see the baby unless he admitted paternity. And she was correct. He had no legal right to see a baby against its mother's wishes unless he admitted to being the baby's father.

He decided to admit paternity and sign relinquishment papers. As soon as he signed, he went to the nursery where he took several pictures of his son.

In most states, if the mother reports that she doesn't know who the father is or if the alleged father cannot be located, court action is still necessary to terminate his parental rights.

"The baby has two parents. The rights of both parents have to be terminated before the child is free for adoption," explained Janice Wills, child welfare worker, Los Angeles County Department of Children's Services. "A presumed father has legal rights; an alleged natural father's rights are determined by the court unless he waives his rights for that determination. That court action is called '7017.'

"Sometimes the father's whereabouts are unknown to the girl," said Ms. Wills, "but every effort is made to locate him. We use whatever information the young woman can remember. His last known address? Any relatives? Friends? Neighbors? Occupants on either side of his last address?

"We also request information from the Department of Motor Vehicles. We check DMV records not only in California but also in any other state where the baby's mother thinks the father has or might have lived as an adult.

"If the alleged father is not located, the court grants the 7017 based on the agency's proof of complete search and the girl's detailed statement concerning their relationship.

"Some girls are telling us they don't know who the father is," she commented. "If the natural mother denies knowledge of who the father is, gives us no name, we still have to do a 7017 court action against him as an unknown father. Sometimes we believe she does know who the baby's father is even if she denies it. In such cases, we hold the social worker responsible for using a lot of care.

"If a girl tells me she has no idea who the father is, I try to explain why it is important that we notify him of her plans. We don't want a man coming back later and saying, 'I heard _____ had a baby and we lived together for awhile. If I had known she had that baby, I would have supported it. I intend to do everything I possibly can *to get my baby.*'

"If she gives a baby up for adoption, she wants to be absolutely sure no one can come back later and make an unhappy situation," Ms. Wills concluded.

The California law is an attempt to protect the rights of both birthparents. Charlotte De Armond, formerly with Children's Home Society of California, reports some girls who would prefer to relinquish for adoption are keeping their babies because if they don't, the father says he will. And sometimes the young mother knows this would not be in the best interests of her baby. Yvette explained why she felt this way:

FATHER CAN
STOP ADOPTION

When Yvette told her parents she was pregnant, there was a terrible scene. In fact, her mother demanded she get an abortion. Yvette talked to David, her 17-year-old boyfriend. They decided to go to San Francisco where they could live with David's brother and his family.

For two or three weeks Yvette enjoyed the change. But there wasn't enough money, the house was a mess, and David's two little nephews drove her crazy. She decided to go home.

---

*Maybe motherhood should
be postponed after all.*

Yvette and her mother somehow overcame their differences and became closer than they had ever been. Both her mother and father suggested adoption, but Yvette was adamant. This was her baby and, David or no David, she would raise it.

About a month before her due date, however, Yvette changed her mind. She wanted to play softball this summer. A small thing, perhaps, but if, because of her baby, she couldn't play ball whenever she wanted, what else would she miss during her teen years? She wanted to enjoy her two remaining years of high school, be able to participate in school activities as she had always done. Maybe motherhood should be postponed after all.

Yvette talked to an adoption agency social worker several times. Her mind was made up. She would give up her baby.

The social worker got in touch with David. He had come back to live with his mother, but he and Yvette weren't seeing each other. In fact, Yvette had become thoroughly disenchanted with his lack of interest in school and his current involvement in drugs. She knew their relationship was over.

For two weeks after his first appointment with the social worker, David threatened to keep the baby himself. His mother would help him raise it. However, after several discussions with Yvette, he told her he would sign for relinquishment as soon as the baby was born.

Three weeks later Yvette delivered a seven-pound girl. After a hospital visit from David and his mother, Yvette put in a panic call to her social worker.

"He says if I release the baby he'll take it to court and get custody," wailed Yvette. "The last thing I want is for him and his mother to raise this baby. You know what kind of home they have. She's on welfare and doesn't even take good care of the kids she has. And imagine David taking care of a baby! Can we stop them?"

The social worker consulted her supervisor. Regretfully she told Yvette and her family that they couldn't guarantee the outcome of such a court case. "It's as if we're on shifting sand," she explained. "So much depends on the judge. At one time we could assure a mother that if she had already signed a relinquishment, she could rescind (take it back) if the baby's father won custody. She could still raise the baby herself if she thought the father would be a poor parent.

"Now, however," she continued, "we simply don't know how the judge will decide. The fact that you lived with David that month in San Francisco undoubtedly makes him the 'presumed' father in the eyes of the court. The presumed father has the same rights as the mother."

Yvette decided not to take the risk. She is raising her baby herself.

PROTECTING FATHERS' RIGHTS

Stacey, whose baby's father insisted she "should" raise the baby herself, resented the struggle she had to go through during pregnancy. It was hard enough making the decision to release her baby for adoption. Having to confront Curt and his pastor and defend that decision was extremely frustrating.

However, when she was asked her opinion of the law concerning fathers' rights, she said thoughtfully:

"I feel it is necessary. The father has the right and he should sign the relinquishment papers. It makes it harder for the mother sometimes – I should know! – but you can't just forget about his rights."

If you have decided or are thinking about releasing your baby for adoption, check the law in your state or province. If you are married, of course both you and your husband must sign the papers. A significant number of married couples voluntarily release children for adoption each year, according to adoption statistics.

If you are single, carefully check with an adoption agency on the laws concerning fathers' rights in your area. It is important to you – and to your baby – that the adoption occur as smoothly as possible.

And it is *extremely* important that *all* legal aspects are handled properly.

8

DEALING WITH GRIEF

Is it ever easy to release a baby for adoption? *Of course it's not!*

Releasing a baby for adoption causes emotions similar to those a mother feels if she loses her baby through death. The birthparent will (or should) go through the same kind of grieving process. If she doesn't, if she simply pushes her grief out of her mind and "forgets the whole thing," she may have emotional problems later.

> *" My problem was I didn't grieve. I just stuffed it all down inside me."*

A young woman in Oregon, who hadn't allowed herself to grieve when her baby was placed, described her need to mourn later:

Fifteen years ago I released my baby for adoption. I was 17 when I became pregnant. Everything was very hush-hush back then. I grew up in a strongly religious home, and my pregnancy was a disgrace. We didn't want the neighbors to know, so I went back to Ohio to live. A doctor and his family took me in.

About the only good thing that happened to me that year was that beautiful family. They gave me lots of love and acceptance that I had never had as I was growing up.

I chose to relinquish because I knew that was the only thing I could do. I always knew my decision was right . . . my problem was I didn't grieve. I just stuffed it all down inside me.

I know nothing about my child except its sex and weight. I was in a labor room by myself across from the nursery. I was heavily sedated during labor and delivery. After the baby was born, they took it away immediately. The next day I decided to go to the nursery to see my baby. As I started to look in the window, a nurse shut the blinds and I heard a baby cry. I'll never forget that cry!

As soon as I was able, I returned to Oregon and finished school. I got a job, was married a couple of years later. We have two children now.

Last year I began to realize I had some serious problems — I felt depressed and wasn't handling my life well at all. I went to see my pastor for counseling.

"Of course a mother who gives up her baby grieves."

Lots of feelings have come out in these counseling sessions. This year I've been going through the stages of grief that I skipped fifteen years ago. It was very difficult for me. Sometimes I would call my counselor

*and say, "Why am I crying?" He would suggest that I
might be having a delayed reaction. We would talk
about what was happening and try to deal with it.*

*If you release your child, you need to know about
the grieving process. You will have to go through it.
You should realize what the stages of grief are –
realize it's OK to deny your grief, to be angry, to be
depressed, to feel rejected.*

*And finally, if you go through these stages and you
don't try to bury your grief, you will feel acceptance.
It's OK to have these feelings. That's been so important to me, to work through these feelings no matter
how long it takes.*

Patricia Schwiebert, R.N., co-author of *When Hello
Means Goodbye*, pointed out, "Of course a mother who
gives up her baby grieves. Sometimes we put road blocks
in her way. We say, 'Well, it wouldn't have worked out
anyhow. You're too young to be a mother. You'll feel
better soon.' All of this may be true, but that isn't what she
needs to hear now. She knows it is *better* or she wouldn't

have made this decision, but she is grieving nevertheless.

"She has already bonded with her baby before birth. Right now she is grieving because she lost her child. You support her feelings at this point. Sometimes we have gotten girls together who are relinquishing and others who did so in the past. They can share how they feel," Ms. Schwiebert concluded.

SEEING BABY BEFORE ADOPTION

Jodie mentioned she hadn't grieved a great deal. Unexpectedly, she took her baby home for two days because she couldn't reach her adoption worker on Christmas Day. She hadn't planned even to see her son:

I didn't really grieve except for the first couple of days. I was fine until I had to start getting his things ready for the adoption worker. It was time to feed him and I couldn't make myself do it. So my sister took over, and I know it was hard on her too. She said, "We'll just think of him as if he's dead."

"I will not think of him that way," I said. "He's not dead, and we won't write him off as if he were."

I knew that he would be better off where he was going. I had placed him in God's hands, and I knew He wouldn't fail me. It was through my faith that I did it. I don't believe I would have made it on my own.

---

*Seeing the baby
reinforces whatever decision
she has already made.*

Caring for her baby those two days was undoubtedly an emotionally healthy situation for Jodie, hard as it was for her. This gave her "closure" in the act of adoption. It made her baby very real to her, and her grieving, while short-lived, was intense.

Janice Wills, a Los Angeles County caseworker, agrees that seeing the baby before it is released for adoption is emotionally healthy. She thinks it completes the adoption in a positive way. "The baby is not a stranger," she commented. "She has carried that baby all this time.

"Sometimes a girl will say that if she sees her baby, she won't be able to give it up. This hasn't happened in my experience. I think seeing the baby reinforces whatever decision she has already made." Ms. Wills suggests that seeing the baby through the nursery window may be enough for some girls, that feeding the baby for several days can make it extremely hard to give him up.

In open adoption, the birthparent(s) and adoptive parents may have an agreement that the birthparents will receive pictures of their child. The adoptive parents may send photos every month or two during the baby's first year, then perhaps on the child's birthday each year. Seeing these photos, knowing her child appears happy and well will help the birthmother cope better with her grief.

"When the birthmother sees the adoptive family with the baby and understands that this once-hurting couple now is a family, she knows she has given a wonderful gift. I think seeing their joy helps to diminish her pain," explained Jennifer Stebbins, Pregnancy Counselor, Christian Adoption and Family Service, Anaheim, California.

"We encourage birthmothers to bring their own cameras to the hospital, to save the identification card off the baby's bassinet, keep the wrist bands, press the flowers. I encourage her family and friends to send her flowers just as they would if she were keeping the baby. I especially encourage the adoptive family to give her flowers and/or a gift. The birthmother will treasure every one of these things," Ms. Stebbins concluded.

The roughest time for Wendi Sue was the first two weeks after delivery. She remembers:

I left the hospital and started crying. I went home and my mom said, "You've been crying." I said, "No," and then I started all over again. My mom was real supportive, but I know the adoption was hard on her and my dad, too. Mandy was their first grandchild and they accepted what I did. They accepted it well.

I was crying in the hospital the night after she was born. The woman in the next bed said, "If it hurts that much, why are you giving her away?" I couldn't explain to her right then, but I knew that something can hurt a lot and still be the right thing to do. When you're hurting, you can still know you did something right. It's not a bad hurt.

HURTING DOESN'T MEAN IT'S WRONG DECISION

If we do something that hurts a lot, we tend to think the act must be wrong. A birthmother may think, "I'm feeling terrible. If it hurts to release my baby for adoption, why should I do it? It must be a poor decision."

Carrying out an adoption plan is an extremely difficult thing to do. If you decide to release your baby for adoption, of course you'll hurt. You need to realize, and your family needs to realize, that this is absolutely normal. It does not mean you're making a poor decision.

While you're pregnant, the adoption plan may make a lot of sense to you. After delivery, however, you may feel confused. You may wonder, "How can I do this?"

While you're pregnant, write the reasons you're making the adoption plan. Is it because you feel you aren't yet ready to parent? Do you want your child to have a different life than you can provide right now? Are you single and you'd like your baby to be in a two-parent home? Make a list of *your* reasons. Put it in your hospital bag.

After your child is born, get out your list. Other people will probably be giving you lots of advice, but your own thinking is most important as you make your final decision. The reasons you were planning adoption are probably still there. At least you can balance them with the feelings you encounter as you spend time with your baby.

YOUR RIGHTS AS A BIRTHPARENT

In years past, a birthmother who made an adoption plan usually didn't see her baby. It was released to the adoptive parents and she was supposed to forget the whole thing.

Today, most people working with birthparents who relinquish recommend that the mother see her baby before she releases. If you plan to release your baby, you may find, however, that someone – perhaps a friend, a nurse in the hospital, possibly even your doctor – tells you *not* to go near the baby, not to see him.

Be sure you make your own decision on this issue, too.

Above all, face the grief you'll surely feel. Don't hide it and refuse to deal with it.

If you consider an adoption plan, you need to know your rights as a birthparent. You have a right to see your baby and to care for your baby as much as you wish while you're in the hospital. Until you sign the adoption papers, your rights are the same as those of any other mother.

If you can't make a decision in the hospital, you have the option of foster care for a short time while you make up your mind. If you decide to keep your baby, you need to remember that adoption will still be available two days

from now . . . or a year from now.

You may be convinced it is better not to see your child. That's OK. But if you're not sure, you'll probably be better off looking at her, perhaps holding her.

If you see her, if she is "real" to you, this can help put "closure" on the adoption. It can help you realize you are truly releasing your baby to the adoptive parents.

If *you* know you don't want, couldn't bear to see and hold your baby, explain your thinking to the hospital personnel. You have a right to decide for yourself.

Above all, face the grief you'll surely feel. Don't hide it in the back of your mind and refuse to deal with it.

When and if you decide on an adoption plan, you may find you go through the pain of "deciding" more than once. While you're pregnant, perhaps you'll "know" it's the best thing to do. After you deliver, you'll wonder if you're doing the right thing. And when you sign the final papers, you'll hurt again.

You may wonder as you face the final signing of the adoption papers, "Why do I still hurt so much? If this is the right decision, should it *hurt*?"

Of course you'll hurt! You're losing a baby. But the hurt will gradually go away – as long as you face your grief and don't try to bury it.

The best "therapy" while in this situation – you're hurting and you wonder if it will ever stop – is to talk with another birthmother who carried out her adoption plan. Perhaps someone who released her baby several years ago will share with you how she feels now about her decision. Not that you will ever feel exactly like someone else, but it often helps to share experiences.

You may also find it helps to write your child a letter telling her how much you love her. You can let her know that it's precisely for that reason you're letting someone else love and care for her.

Or you may prefer to write to your baby's adoptive family. Whether or not you meet them, your letter could mean a lot to them and to your/their child.

Final signing for relinquishment can be soon after you leave the hospital if you're releasing to an agency. Or it may be two months after your baby has been independently placed in an adoptive home. (Remember, the public agency in most states will do a home study after the baby is placed in independent adoption.)

If the adoption is closed, either the adoptee or the birth-parent may search for the other later. Ms. Stebbins reports that almost all ("99 percent") of her agency's birthparent clients are open to contact when the child reaches adult-hood. Birthparents usually sign a paper to this effect when they're signing the final adoption papers.

FATHERS GRIEVE TOO

Often the baby's father needs to grieve too. I understood this when I visited Ellen who had relinquished her baby a year earlier. To my surprise, her baby's father was there when I arrived. I hadn't realized they were seeing each other again.

Carl appeared upset as Ellen talked. He played nervously with the bracelets she had taken from her arm. He looked alert, smiled at the right places as she told her story, but occasionally he appeared close to tears.

Ellen's mother had explained quietly that Carl was back in the picture. To her amazement, she and Ellen's father thought the world of him.

When Ellen was pregnant, her baby's father was almost
never mentioned. At that time her mother had told me
Ellen didn't know his name. As I had guessed at the time, I
soon learned this wasn't so. However, he and Ellen didn't
see each other during her pregnancy, and I assumed he was
gone.

---

*He seemed depressed,
burdened with guilt feelings.*

Ellen's lawyer had gotten Carl's signature for waiver of
his rights in the adoption proceeding. At the time, because
of parental pressure, Ellen would have nothing to do with
him. His parents had moved across town, and he had
enrolled in another high school. He was 16, a tenth grader,
and he was trying to forget the whole mess.

When the lawyer called, Carl was scared. He was told
rapidly of his rights, with the added comment that the
waiver would be the "simplest" unless, of course, he
wanted to deny paternity. He signed the waiver.

A year later he saw Ellen again. They started dating, and
soon reestablished their close relationship. As I talked with
Ellen, she urged me to include him in the interview. I
hesitated, not wanting to pry, not wanting to hurt him. Then
we started talking.

While Ellen was sure she had made the right decision in
releasing the baby for adoption, Carl obviously was not so
sure. He seemed depressed, burdened with guilt feelings.
As he talked, it became evident he had not shared his
feelings about the adoption with anyone. Ellen was so sure
of the rightness of the adoption – how could he burden her
with his feelings of loss?

"Just talking about this today is impressive," he said.
"Somehow I feel better."

Fathers often experience *denial* of grief more intensely
and for a longer period of time that do the mothers. This

may give others (and themselves) the impression that they aren't experiencing any effects from the loss of the baby.

Apparently Carl had not allowed himself to grieve while the adoption was taking place. Only now, many months later, was he facing his loss and dealing with it.

Often the father, as in Carl's situation, is simply behind time in his grieving. He may not experience the reality of the child until birth occurs. To the mother, the child was real throughout pregnancy, and her feelings of parenthood become even more intense at birth. If her child is released for adoption, she will grieve. The father may not . . . until later.

POEM BY GIBRAN MAY HELP BIRTHPARENT

Whenever you're hurting, perhaps especially at the final signing, you may think, "This is my baby, it's part of me." A poem by Kahlil Gibran may help:

> *And a woman who held a babe against*
> *her bosom said, Speak to us of Children.*
> *And he said:*
> *Your children are not your children.*
> *They are the sons and daughters*
> *of Life's longing for itself.*
> *They come through you but not*
> *from you,*
> *And though they are with you*
> *yet they belong not to you.*
>
> *You may give them your love but not*
> *your thoughts,*
> *For they have their own thoughts.*
> *You may house their bodies but not*
> *their souls,*

For their souls dwell in the house of tomorrow,
which you cannot visit, not even in your dreams.
You may strive to be like them, but seek
not to make them like you
For life goes not backward nor tarries
with yesterday.

You are the bows from which your children
as living arrows are sent forth.
The archer sees the mark upon the path
of the infinite, and He bends you with His
might that His arrows may go swift and far.
Let your bending in the archer's hand
be for gladness;
For even as He loves the arrow that flies,
so He loves also the bow that is stable.

The Prophet by Kahlil Gibran
1963: Alfred A. Knopf, Inc., pages 17-18.

As Gibran says, our children are not ours, they go through us. This thought applies not only to all parents generally, but perhaps especially to birthparents who are allowing someone else to parent their child.

9

BIRTHPARENTS WRITE LETTERS

If you're considering an adoption plan, you may want to write a letter to your baby. Many birthmothers and some birthfathers find this helps them deal with the pain of losing their baby.

If you're working out a plan with the adoptive parents so that you can see pictures of your child occasionally, even visit him/her, a letter may still be important to you and your baby. Ginny wants her son to read her letter to him (see below) when he is 18. Other birthmothers suggest that the adoptive parents read the letter to their child when s/he is small.

In a "closed" agency adoption, a letter from a birthmother to her child is usually placed in the agency file until the time the birthmother wants the adoptive parents to receive it. The agency will then contact the child's adoptive parents and give them the letter.

"Before I even felt you move,
I loved you and wanted you
to have the best."

Birthparents considering an adoption plan for their baby
tend to worry that their child might think they didn't love
him. Will he assume they "gave him away" because they
didn't want him? Usually, of course, the opposite is true –
they chose adoption for their child *because* they love him
and want a better life for him than they can provide.
Through a letter, Ginny, 16, explained:

Dear Son,
    This is the most painful letter I've ever had to write.
I wish I hadn't put it off for so long. I've started it so
many times but could never find the right words to tell
you how much you mean to me.
    I think the first thing you should know is both your
father and I love you very much. Don't ever doubt
that. We both wanted more for you than we were able
to give.
    The decision to let go was not made easily or
hastily. It took months of soul-searching and going
back and forth on decisions. Finally, it came down to
actually signing the forms. Even though it wasn't the
decision we wanted to make, we knew we couldn't do
any better for you.
    I love your father and I believe he feels the same
about me. I feel we have something that's going to
last. We weren't ready to become parents when you
came along but someday we hope to have more chil-
dren together (when we're ready to give them the love,
the time, and the comfort of a happy home). You will
always be a part of our family and if someday you
would like to come back into our lives there will be a
place for you.

Son, I wish all the best for you. Most of all, I wish
you peace, love, wisdom and understanding. Open
your heart as well as your mind and you will have all
that really matters.

Love to you always,
Your birthmother

CYNDI SHARES HER FEELINGS

Dear Travis,

*It's not easy writing this but I feel you need to
know why I placed you for adoption. Since before I
even felt you move, I loved you and wanted you to
have the best. The way I feel about life and children is
that a child needs a mother and a father to guide, care
for, and spend the time needed to rear a child to be
happy and full of love for others. I have the love that is
required, but time is my downfall. My resources are
limited and my time is minimal.*

*I chose to place you because I wanted my son to
have a mother who would love him and spend the time
to set values and morals that are scarce today.*

*I chose to place you because I wanted my son to
have a father to guide him and be there for him when
he needed the reassurance of a man.*

*But most of all I chose to place you because you are
so special to me. You deserve more than I have to
offer. I hope that someday I will feel myself worthy to
raise a child in the proper way.*

*For the rest of my life I will feel regrets for not
being the one to share your joys and sorrows, for not
being the one to advise you when you approach a
dilemma, and for not being the one to watch you
achieve your goals.*

Travis, I know that I have given you a chance, a chance to have a father who loves you, a chance to receive the all-day care of a mother, a chance to grow in a home where love is important and shared, a chance to receive a good education and be whatever you want to be. Whatever that may be, my prayers are with you.

"Never let anyone tell you I did not love you. It was because of my deep, deep love for you that I let you go!"

Whenever you feel the time is right to seek me out, don't be afraid to do so. My arms will always be open to you but don't worry that I will in any way pressure you to see me.

You have your family now, a family who loves you as their own. They are very lucky to be able to share your life and I know you will grow up to have a strong set of morals and responsibilities.

Never let anyone tell you that I did not love you because it was my deep, deep love for you that I let you go! I will remember always the time that you and I spent together, and the love we shared will always be there!

I love you.

Cyndi

Cyndi didn't meet Travis' adoptive parents, but she felt she knew them. Her social worker described several families and she chose the Millers because they seemed most like her own family. She felt they would parent Travis as she wanted him parented.

As soon as she heard Travis was born, Carole Miller wrote to Cyndi:

Dear Birthmother,

It is very important to us that you know how much joy you've let into our lives by allowing us to raise your very special son. We have hoped and prayed and dreamed of having a child for four years now. God chose you to make our dream come true, and we love you for that.

We understand how difficult it must be for you to let go of someone you love because you love him. We hope it will ease your pain to know that he will know of the love you have for him and the tremendous sacrifice you made.

We know this first year will be a difficult one for you. Just remember that we love you very much, but most of all, God loves you and he is always there for you. We hope it is a comfort to you that while he is looking after you, he is also looking after your son.

The first child is always special, so this little boy is

extra special since he is your first and ours. We know you will never forget him, and in return, we will never forget you. You will be in our prayers all the days of our lives.

There are so many things we want to do for him. He will grow up knowing God loves him. We want to help him develop his talents and grow to be a loving and courageous man. We want, as you do, only the best for him.

Though we have not as yet had him in our arms, we love this little boy with all our hearts. We feel so special that we were chosen to see him through life. Thank you.

Your son's adoptive parents

Cyndi spent a great deal of time with Travis while they were in the hospital. A few days after she received the Millers' letter, she responded:

Dear Parents of Travis,

I love you both for being so wonderful and giving love to my child. I am thankful that there are people in this world who are kind, loving and responsible and can love another person's child as their own. I know that you will love Travis because anyone who holds that wonderful child will love him. I thank God for the time I was able to spend with him. The memory of his first three days of life will be etched in my heart forever.

I would like both of you to know that although my love for Travis is very deep, I would never jeopardize his happiness by trying to take him away from you. My decision to place him for adoption was a rational one and I could never change it now. I don't want you to feel you have to be cautious with your new son because you fear I will try to take him away from you.

He is part of me but he is also part of you and your
love for him is vital to his happiness.

I would like to express my great desire to hear from
you often on the progress of my son's life. It is so im-
portant to me to know how he is doing and growing.
I pray that you both will feel free to write and send
pictures as often as you can.

I don't want ever to forget my son. To share a small
portion of his life with you would give me so much
pleasure! I cry for the loss of my first-born, but I'm
also happy for him because he is receiving all the love
a child deserves.

My family and I grieve for our loss and share the
need to know how he is doing.

I love you both.

Cyndi

ANOTHER BIRTHMOTHER WRITES TO ADOPTIVE PARENTS

Anne and her sister, Rachel, were very close. When Anne, 18, became pregnant, she and Rachel were living together. They were attending college about 300 miles from their parents' home.

Anne was able to continue attending classes until the end of her freshman year, then two weeks later gave birth to Christi. With lots of support from her sister and the baby's father, Anne released the baby for adoption.

Anne chose her child's christening dress. Rachel bought tiny shoes for Christi. With these gifts Anne sent a letter to the baby's adoptive parents:

Dear Friends,
Even though we have never met, I feel close to you
both. We share someone very precious. I love my
daughter very much, and it was so hard to give her up.

But I know you will be good parents to her.

Did you know she was born on her father's birth-day? I would like her to know that. I'd also like you to save the dress and shoes. The shoes are from my sister.

If you don't mind, I would love updated pictures of Christi. Please know I will never try to take her away from you. You are her family now. But she is a part of me I don't want to forget. With pictures, I can watch her grow into the beautiful young lady we both know she will be. Please consider my request.

Thank you so much for the gifts. They brightened my day.

Give Christi a kiss for me. Take care of her and yourselves.

> *Love,*
> *Your friend*

Three weeks later Anne received several pictures of her daughter together with this letter:

Dear Birthmother of Christi,

I want to tell you how very much we appreciate the sacrifice you have made. As a mother I know how very difficult this decision must have been. We will love and cherish this greatest gift from you.

We have two sons but I've always wanted a daughter. I haven't been able to have children for nine years. My heart has felt an emptiness and great sorrow at times because of this. You have mended our heartache.

My husband and I love children and your baby is filling our lives with joy and happiness. We promise to give her a good life, full of love and much attention.

I hope this helps you to continue to feel confident in your decision.

Our boys will adore her and treat her like a princess. You'll be remembered in our hearts for this great deed and you'll be in our prayers.

Christi's adoptive parents

FATHER WRITES LETTER

Rafael was deeply involved in the adoption planning for his son. He and Bryan's mother read at least a dozen descriptions of families before making their decision. Soon after Bryan was born, Rafael wrote the following letter to him:

To my son,

A few days ago I watched an all-too-young girl of eighteen years give birth to a beautiful, healthy baby boy. The life that I watched begin was your own, and I who write this letter am your natural father.

This letter was originally intended to explain some of the reasons your mother and I felt it would be best if we placed you for adoption, but I hope it can be more than that. I hope that when you read these words in twenty years you will be able to understand some of the feelings that I am trying to express and sense me as a person behind them.

As I write this, you lie in the hospital only a few days old. I am nineteen. I have my hopes and dreams, my fears and sorrows as all men do. A year ago I would have called myself an idealist. Now I think I am more of a realist.

Though you were born into a sad world you need not add to that sadness. Be your own man, and choose your own way. Find your true self within you and recognize your needs and motives. Develop your mind to its fullest: your thoughts, your ideas, your ability to reason. These all make up your soul.

"Though you were unexpected, you were not unwanted."

Let me tell you a little bit about how you came into being.

I met your mother about a year before you were born. We were both freshmen in college at the time. It was a wonderful carefree time, and we fell in love so fast that I do not remember ever knowing her and not loving her.

It was very easy to fall in love with your mother. She warms my soul like the morning sun. Her laughing green eyes are windows into her gentle inner self. If I had to describe her in one word, it would be grace. Grace of body and mind, grace of self and spirit. You are the product of our love, you are the offspring of our happiness.

Though you were unexpected, you were not un-wanted. We wanted to keep you and raise you. But in our love for you we knew that we could only do for you what we thought was best for you. We are not ready to raise a child, and I believe that you would have suffered had we tried.

I was with your mother all through her labor, and I witnessed your birth. I loved you when you were born, and I will love you all your life. I hope fate is kind to you, and I hope that beauty and love will surround you, for they are perfect things in our imperfect world.

Your father

LEEANN'S PLANS CHANGE

When LeeAnn realized, two months before her sixteenth birthday, that she was pregnant, she was both frightened and excited. Her boyfriend, Jim, was thrilled. He had dropped out of school to work in a fast-food place. He said he would take care of LeeAnn and the baby.

For several months LeeAnn went along with his plans. The day they started looking for a place to live, however, it became obvious to both of them that they couldn't afford to live by themselves. They would have to stay with LeeAnn's mom who had said she would help them. But she was already supporting LeeAnn and three other children by herself, and LeeAnn didn't see how their tiny house could expand much more.

At first, when she mentioned adoption as a possibility, Jim exploded. No one was going to take his baby away from him. Then he, too, started thinking about their realities.

As they talked, he realized he wasn't ready to support a baby. He and LeeAnn decided they wanted more for their child than they could offer him.

They chose a family through their adoption agency counselor. Alex was born December 23. He went home with his adoptive parents on Christmas Day. LeeAnn wrote the following letter to him:

> *To my son,*
>
> *I love you. Those are just three tiny words, but they hold more meaning from me to you than anything I've ever said. There is no possible way I could express all the love I feel for you.*
>
> *I gave you up for adoption because I wanted you to have more than I did and I couldn't give that to you. I was only sixteen when I had you. All I could give you was your life and then place you in the hands of people who can give you what you deserve.*
>
> *I grew up without a father so my mother has always worked and couldn't spend any time with us. She supported four kids, two boys and two girls, by herself. With all the time she worked we still didn't have much.*

*That's how it would have been for you. Now you have
a father and a mother who can spend time with you.
You're very lucky.*

*When you were born and I saw you for the first time
all I could do was laugh and say, "Isn't he beautiful?"
Your grandmother was there through labor and
delivery. When she saw you, she cried. She's a wonderful lady and if you're lucky, you'll inherit some of
her qualities.*

*I held and fed you while we were in the hospital.
You looked just like your father. Christmas Day I left
the hospital. That's the hardest thing I've ever done in
my life, and probably the saddest day I'll ever have.*

*I think about you every day, every minute. I love you
so much, and I wish you a very happy life.*

God bless.

Your birthmother

LeeAnn also wrote to her baby's adoptive parents:

Dear Parents,

*I feel really good about this adoption. You can give
that little baby so much more than I can. I believe that
it was meant to be. This will probably be the hardest
thing I'll ever do in my life. It's so hard, but I'm doing
it out of love. I love him more than I've ever loved
anyone or anything in my life. He'll always be my
first-born – my child. It's just that God has put him in
your care. One child can have three parents.*

*I want to thank you for the diaper changing, late-
night feedings, taking care of small or large colds, etc.
But could you thank God for the first smiles, the first
time he rolls over or sits up, the challenges he over-
comes in life? I know that you'll love him and take
good care of him. I wish I could be the one to do these
things, but I guess it wasn't meant to be.*

I want to say thank you and I also thank God that he
put my baby in the care of two wonderful people.
Merry Christmas and take good care of him.
                                                    Birthmother (16)

KEY RING IS SYMBOL OF BABY'S LOVE

Shawna's baby's adoptive parents were especially sensitive to Shawna's need to feel close to her child even though she couldn't be with him. They found two key rings which, put together, contained a message which they included in the following letter:

Dear Mother,
   Please accept this key ring as a token of my love.
Someday, if it be God's will, I will personally present
you with my key ring and the two together will read:
"The Lord watch between me and thee while we are
absent one from another." Genesis 31:49.

Also, please continue to remember me in your
prayers and I will be taught always to pray, asking
God to be with you.

                              Your son, Sean
     P.S. I love you!

Separately, the message was incomplete. Sean's adoptive
parents took a picture of the baby holding a key ring in
each tiny hand. Beneath the photo was written, "First they
were mine. Now they are ours. Later they will be yours."
They sent the picture, one key ring, and the following
letter to Shawna:

Although we have never met, our lives have been
beautifully interwoven because of our mutual love for
a precious little boy named Sean.
     May the peace of God be with you.

                              Sean's family

If you decide on an adoption plan for your baby, you may
find writing a letter to him/her will help you deal with your
grief. Sharing your feelings with your child and with his/
her adoptive parents is important for your peace of mind
and for your child's.
Your letter will be very precious to your child as s/he
matures. It will be cherished by his/her new family as a
symbol of your love.

10

RELEASING TODDLER FOR ADOPTION

WHO AM I?

By Tanelle Garrison, 15-Year-Old Mother

I'm not sure who I am.
Maybe you can help me.
Am I a lost little girl . . .
Or a grown woman?
Surely you can help me.

Yes, maybe I'll find who I am . . .
Maybe I won't.
And if by chance I don't,
Maybe you can help me.

What will happen if I never find who I am?
Will I die . . . or will I live . . .
Am I a lost litttle girl
Or a grown woman?
Maybe I will never know.

Tannelle speaks for many school-age mothers. If a girl becomes a mother before she finds who she is herself, she may start wondering, "Who am I? Am I 'just' a mother? How do I have a life of my own now?"

The young mother with these thoughts may be a very "good" mother. Tanelle certainly is. So was Lorraine. She shared her story of her two years with Luke:

> *I didn't consider adoption before delivery because my boyfriend didn't want me to. At first, it was a pretty good experience, being a mother. I loved him, and I still do.*
>
> *That spring was neat. I was really into motherhood. Summer was OK, although I missed going to the beach every day as I used to do. Then I started dating and got back into basketball. I was so pleased when I lettered last year.*

When he was about eight months old, I told my mom I was thinking of giving him up.

> *Times got harder. I have a sister a year older than I am. Seeing her free to go out whenever she wanted was difficult to take.*
>
> *I started going out a lot, too, and I'd leave Luke with my mom. I started thinking, "I'm not even taking care of him."*
>
> *Then it got still harder to cope with him. When he was about eight months old, I told my mom I was thinking of giving him up.*
>
> *She was all broken up, so I didn't talk about it again for a long time. But the idea of adoption kept going through my mind.*
>
> *It was about a year later that I brought up adoption again. I had talked with a girlfriend who has a child*

Luke's age. She's married, but she really understood how I felt. She told me I should do it if that's what I wanted.

So I talked with my family. My sister's boyfriend knew a couple who wanted to adopt a little boy. She couldn't have any kids because she had had a hysterectomy.

Sam told me all about them, and then I met them. We sat and talked for a long time. Luke started spending weekends with them and he adapted amazingly well, we thought.

About two months later I signed the adoption papers. My mother still sees Luke. His adoptive mother never had a father, and she had always said she would welcome Luke's birthgrandparents. I see them once in awhile too.

Sometimes I cry when I'm down because I miss him. I learned, though, that it's best to go by what you feel. Don't let anybody talk you out of what you want to do. Don't listen to other people.

You have to live with yourself. Just do what you feel is right for you and for your baby.

Life hasn't been easy for Lorraine. Losing a son who is almost two years old is probably a great deal harder than losing a baby.

Sure, bonding occurs during pregnancy, and giving up a baby is difficult, but Lorraine and Luke shared a lot in the time they had together. It took a great deal of courage (and some desperation) for Lorraine to do what she knew was best for her and for Luke.

She called recently. She said she still enjoys school and will graduate in two months.

She sees Luke occasionally. In fact, she had taken him shopping the day before she called.

CHILD'S AGE
AT RELINQUISHMENT

Like Lorraine, young birthmothers sometimes find parenting becomes too difficult a couple of years after delivery. They may wonder, "Is adoption still an option?"

The Los Angeles Department of Children's Services places many children in adoptive homes each year. Far fewer than one-third of these children are adopted as infants. It is only later, after experiencing the difficulties of parenting, that some young parents voluntarily, others involuntarily, release their children for adoption.

---

*They start thinking about the
tremendous responsibility
of raising a child after they
leave home.*

An example of the heartbreak in later placement is the letter a social worker received from a young mother who had relinquished two toddlers. "Please have a happy life. I hope you'll know me some day," she wrote. The letter, addressed to her children, will go in their file. It will be there for them when they are grown.

A Children's Home Society counselor commented, "We're seeing teen mothers who, perhaps because of family pressure, decided to keep their babies. Now a year or two later, some are coming back to discuss adoption.

"Sometimes they really start thinking about the tremendous responsibility of raising a child after they leave home and are living by themselves. Sometimes a boyfriend doesn't want an instant family."

MICHELE'S LIFE CHANGES

At first Michele enjoyed parenting. Caring for her infant daughter went smoothly for awhile. A few months later, however, she found it hard to cope with the damands of constant motherhood:

Remember how furious I was with my family most of the time I was pregnant? I had had it up to here with my mom and dad, our church, everything. I didn't mean to get pregnant – at least, I don't think I did. But in a way I probably wanted to show them I didn't have to be the person they wanted me to be.

I wanted to be such a good mother. I loved working in the Infant Center while I was pregnant, and that Parent Psychology class was my favorite.

The first two or three months after Sharon was born were great. She was such a good baby. Sure, I had to get up in the middle of the night at first, but I didn't really mind. All she seemed to need then was to eat and sleep.

But then things changed.

"Things" had indeed changed. When Sharon was three months old, Michele had gotten involved again with friends

who were into drugs. She didn't seem to care about herself anymore – she didn't eat much, got terribly thin.

Michelle started making comments about her own lack of worth, what a poor mother she was. She lived with her mother part of the time, and moved in with her boyfriend periodically.

> *I began to think Sharon wasn't getting what she needed. I didn't want to take care of her physical needs, but I knew I had to. And emotionally I realized I just wasn't cutting it.*

Michele talked of the time she hit bottom and knew she had to do something about Sharon. Finally she called Pat from Children's Home Society. They talked a long time. She explained to Pat that motherhood somehow wasn't working for her.

She was tired of responsibility. She was tired of the hard work. She missed her freedom to come and go as she wished.

Pat came back the next day. She described a young family who lived near the beach. They had learned a year earlier that they could never have a child born to them, and they wanted to adopt.

It was scary, thinking of Sharon, and having the power to choose a new family for her.

The mother had been working in an insurance agency. She had recently quit her job to stay home and get ready for the adopted baby they hoped to have soon. The father had a good job.

Both enjoyed the beach and sailing in their small boat. They wanted to share their lives with a child. Michele continued her story:

*Pat let me read their file. It was scary, thinking of
Sharon, and having the power to choose a new family
for her. When I looked at what I was giving her, and
then at what this family could offer, I knew I had to do
it. I loved her too much to keep on the way we'd been
going.*

Michele had several more counseling sessions with Pat.
She decided to sign the adoption papers. She wrote a letter
to Sharon and asked Pat to give it to her daughter's new
parents.

Pat did so, and Michele received a short, unsigned note a
few weeks later, a letter she keeps in the album with
Sharon's baby pictures:

*Thank you for the greatest gift anyone could ever
give us. Sharon already is adjusting to her new home,
and we love her.*

*We're already telling her about her first mother
who, because she loved her, decided to let us become
her new parents and love and care for her.*

*We love your/our daughter very much – and we love
you.*

Michele commented later:

*I think Sharon helped me get myself together. I know
she's OK where she is. We had our time together, and now
I must get on with my life.*

Michele graduated from high school four months after
the adoption. She has a job she enjoys, and a new boyfriend. They're getting married this winter.

A single mother of a two- or three-year-old usually has a
much more difficult time deciding on adoption than does a
mother of a newborn. This is due in part to family and peer
pressures.

She and her child have shared many common experiences with her family and friends. These people have a great deal of influence on her decision, and they need to be supportive in whatever her choice may be.

She is likely to spend many hours painfully considering her alternatives. She knows her child is growing and has some needs she can't meet, especially if she's young and in the welfare cycle. Sometimes she can't see a way out unless she remembers adoption.

PHYLLIS SAYS SHE'S MOTHER TOO SOON

Phyllis finds motherhood difficult. Her life with her small daughter is not satisfying. She shared her feelings:

I was living with my mother when I found I was pregnant. I didn't mean to get pregnant, but when it happened, I figured this would be a good way to get out of the house. My mom and I weren't getting along at all then.

First Steve and I ran away to Eugene (Oregon), but I didn't like it there. We came back and moved in with Steve's parents. That didn't work either, so two weeks before Heather was born, we got our own apartment.

Steve got a job, so I went off welfare – but he was always getting fired. I didn't want to go back on welfare. Anyway, I couldn't because I was living with Steve and he was working part of the time. Lots of times we didn't even have money for food. It was really awful.

"It's just no fun any more.
Life is a drag."

*After Heather was born I lost contact with my
friends. I see almost nobody, none of the people I used
to hang around with before I had Heather. I don't
really have friends I can go out with now, so I'm by
myself most of the time. Steve was always out with his
friends drinking beer and partying. I couldn't go with
him because there was no one to watch Heather.*

*Finally I moved back with my mom three months
ago. Steve and I just weren't getting along. We still
aren't. I had hoped my mom would help me out by
watching Heather sometimes. But she tells me she just
got through raising kids – she doesn't have time now.
Some girls like to stay home and take care of a baby,
but I think it's hard. There's nobody I can even talk to
that really tells me how they feel. Everybody says it's
fun, it's great being a mother. I don't agree.*

*Everybody was so nice to me when I was pregnant.
They said, "Oh, I can't wait until you have it. I'll
babysit for you." Then as soon as I had her, nobody
seemed to care. They didn't pay any attention at all to*

*me and Heather any more. It's hard finding somebody
to babysit – even when I have the money for it. I'd like
to go out but I can't.*

*It's just no fun any more. Life is a drag. There's
nothing to live for but just to struggle. People tell me
I'm still young and have my whole life ahead of me,
but I want to have fun now. It's routine every day – I
get up in the morning, take Heather to school, go to
school myself, then come home and struggle with
Heather.*

"Did you ever consider adoption?"

*Yes, when Heather was about five months old I
thought about it. I talked to my mom and she said,
"Oh, you could never do something like that." She
didn't seem to think at all about how I felt. She worried mostly about what other people would think. She
said, "You made your mistake and you have to live
with it."*

*I still think about adoption, but I keep thinking it
will be easier when she gets older. Maybe I can take
care of her then. But I've been tied down since I was
16, and I haven't had time to do anything I want to do.
All I can see ahead of me are problems. It's just too
much responsibility for a young girl.*

"How would you change your life if you could?"

*Not have a child right now. Have a boyfriend,
somebody that cares about me. Just to have somebody.
Having Heather limits me a lot with guys.*

*If I gave Heather up, I wouldn't have anybody. I
couldn't even talk to my mom. Everybody would look
down on me and say, "How could you do that?"*

*I don't know whether I could do it – give her up
now. Of course I love her a lot, but sometimes I think*

she'd be better off with parents a little older and ready to settle down.

I don't know what to do.

SUSIE AND ED CHOOSE A FAMILY

Susie was (is) an adorable girl, very bright. Her large family is deeply involved in the Methodist Church. She was a cheerleader at her high school.

Her family didn't like her boyfriend at all. They were convinced he was a loser and that their daughter deserved better.

When Susie, 16, told her parents she was pregnant, they hit the roof. So she and Ed ran away. She soon learned, to her disappointment, that Ed, too, was less than happy about the pregnancy. But they continued living together.

When she was seven months pregnant, Susie enrolled in the special class for pregnant students. She had passed her high school proficiency exam, but she decided to come to school because of the prepared childbirth instruction, prenatal health discussions, and the parenting class.

One day she commented:

I'm not sure I'm ready to be a mother, especially since Ed doesn't really want a baby. But I'll not decide until it's born.

Susie did choose to keep Letitia – until she was nine months old. She finally decided at that time to release her daughter for adoption.

A year later she shared her experiences with the students in the special class:

I feel giving up Letitia was the best possible decision for all of us. I'm still in contact with her and with her family. I know this is unusual, but for me, it's best. Especially now, during the holiday season, I have to know what's going on with her life.

"Ed and I weren't getting along. He wasn't ready to be a father, and I thought our relationship was ending."

People ask how I could do this, how I could give her up after being her mother for nine months. Well, I feel I was a very good mother, but I was able to put her in a home with a better atmosphere. I gave her to people who are raising her even better than I was.

It was like an answer to prayer the day my mother's friend called. I was feeling low, and I started talking to her. I was crying, and suddenly she said, "Susie, I know a family who might be interested in adopting Letitia. Let me call them and see how they feel." I told her to go ahead.

Two hours later she called me back and said, "These people want to meet you and Letitia, and they're interested in adopting her." Then she told me more about them.

I had already heard of them through my mom and dad who knew them. They had two adopted children, five and eight years old.

LETITIA MEETS HER NEW FAMILY

Ed, Letitia, and I went over to see them. At that time Ed and I weren't getting along. He wasn't ready to be a father, and I thought our relationship was ending. I knew I didn't want to raise Letitia by myself.

We talked with them and with their children for hours. We were really impressed. They were down-to-earth people, family oriented, and they seemed super excited about taking Letitia. We left her there that day and that night.

We went back each day for four days, and she seemed to be adjusting. It was hard for me. I would go home and cry and cry and think, I can't do this. But I had to bring myself to reality.

When you're pregnant, you get into kind of a fantasy world. You're not realistic. When I was pregnant, I "knew" my family would help me, and that it would get better. But it doesn't. You just have to bring yourself back to reality before you can go ahead and make the decision that's best for you and for your baby.

Anyway, I left Letitia with this family and went to Albuquerque to be with my parents. I think that was the only way I could have left her. If I had stayed here, I simply wouldn't have been strong enough to do it.

"I tell girls thinking of adoption that it's going to hurt. It's going to hurt like Hell."

A woman who lived across the street from my parents' home had released a child several years earlier. We talked a lot and she helped me cope.

Three months later Letitia and her new family came to Albuquerque to visit. They let me take care of Letitia for the whole weekend while they visited friends there. She remembered me a little, and she was absolutely delightful, but she obviously had a new family now.

Six months later I came back to Los Angeles. Ed and I are together again and our relationship is one thousand percent better. A lot of the pressure we had

*felt between us was because of the baby. He just
wasn't ready to be a father, and I know now I wasn't
ready for parenthood either.*

*When I relinquished, I was a peer counselor here in
the Teen Mother Program. A lot of the girls in my
group got married. Only one other girl released for
adoption. She went on to do the things with her life
that she wanted to do.*

*Almost all of the other girls ended up being stuck at
home, getting divorced, and being on welfare. I
thought then, and I still do, that I want more than that
for my baby and myself.*

*Most of the girls I know who have released feel
good about their decision. I tell girls who are thinking
of adoption that it's going to hurt. It's going to hurt
like Hell. I'm not a crier, not especially emotional.
When it comes down to pain, I hold it in but I think it's
important to let people know where you're at with
your feelings.*

SHE'LL NEVER FORGET LETITIA

*Sometimes people think if you're going to relin-
quish, you aren't going to think about it. If you don't
think about it, it will go away. It's not like that. It's
with you for your whole life. If the baby isn't with you
physically, she's in your mind. I think about Letitia
every day, and that's like the other birthmothers I
know who have relinquished a child.*

*There is a complete cycle of grief you must go
through. I don't think you ever finish until you go
ahead and have a wanted baby. When you start the
mothering process and you aren't able to finish it, the
cycle isn't complete.*

I saw Letitia a month ago on Halloween. She's almost two now, and is just a doll. Her mom is a total homemaker. She cooks and sews and does lots of things I don't do, and she and I have a surprisingly good relationship.

I met Letitia's grandparents too. You know, if I had kept her, she wouldn't have all these neat relationships with her brother and sister and with her grandparents.

When you think about parents who are adopting, wow! They're really into it.

You can give your baby as much love as you have. But if you haven't finished growing up yet, that love can never be as much as your baby could have from someone who has been waiting several years for her.

I feel that if you have a child before you've grown up yourself, it's going to be different. No matter how much you think it's going to be OK, that it will be like every other kid, it simply isn't that way. There is still a social stigma against children born to young and single mothers.

You'll have some negative feelings and so will other people. I think the child picks up on this. If you keep the baby, this may affect her whole life.

I feel keeping is sometimes a really selfish decision. When you do this, you aren't thinking about the future. You're thinking about what's easier for you. It's not really easier to keep, but relinquishing is a more difficult decision to make.

This was the hardest thing I have ever done in my life. With anything you do, if it's easy, it won't give you peace of mind. If it's hard, and you know it's right, it will make you feel good.

Four young women who became mothers too soon – sooner than they wanted. Lorraine – Michele – Phyllis – Susie. Phyllis is still agonizing over her future – and her daughter's.

Lorraine – Michele – Susie. Each faced the heartbreak of an adoption plan for the child she loved dearly. Each decided she couldn't cope with motherhood at this point in her life.

Lorraine – Michele – Susie. Each realized when things got rough, she still had a choice. Adoption was still an option for her child.

11

ADOPTEES GROW UP

Were any of your friends adopted? Do you know anyone who has adopted a child?

Many thousands of adoptions occur each year in the United States, and many of these adoptions are infants. More than 10,000 teenagers release babies for adoption annually. You probably know families with adopted children.

For many years most adoptive parents were secretive about their child's adoption. Often the child was not told she was adopted. Novels are published dealing with the plight of the adolescent who suddenly learns she is not her parents' birthchild. Research shows emotional problems often result from such situations.

The problem generally was in the *secret*, not the adoption. How would you feel if for sixteen years you assumed you were born to your parents, then accidentally learned you were adopted?

The fact that your parents kept that information from you would probably hurt – and hurt a lot. You might feel you couldn't trust them any more. If they hadn't been honest with you about something as basic as your birth, you might think they must be dishonest in other things too.

If dishonesty weren't involved, if you'd "always" known you were adopted, would it matter? If you had a good relationship with your parents, what difference would it make to you whether or not you were actually born to them? Janet, 24, sees no difference:

GUESS WHAT?
I'M ADOPTED!

Janet, 24, a lovely brunette, married her high school sweetheart during their senior year at college. They have two children now and Janet teaches art in the local high school. She shared her positive feelings about her adoption:

I was three weeks old when I was adopted. I grew up in a very loving home and have never had any problem thinking of my parents as my parents. To me, they always have been. That's all I've known.

---

*"I've been raised
as if I were very special."*

I can't tell you when I was first told I was adopted. My mom and I have a very open relationship, and we have talked about it a lot. It's as if I have always known. My mom said she and my dad made the decision to tell me before they adopted me because they thought it would be healthier for them and for me.

They had been married for ten years and had been trying to have a baby. Doctors couldn't find anything

wrong with them, but they finally started proceedings
to adopt. It took two years back then. They were told
that if they didn't feel immediate bonding when they
first saw me, not to take me. They felt it!

I've been raised as if I were very special. My
mother told me I was a gift to them from God – especially since there was no reason the doctor could find
for them not to conceive and bear a child. By the time
I was about two, she would bring adoption into our
conversations.

She used to read me stories about parents going to
the hospital to pick up a baby, not to have it born
there. Then she would tell me that was how they got
me, that I didn't come from her tummy. I think it was
this honesty that made me feel so good.

When I was in fourth or fifth grade I asked a lot of
questions. About that time Mom also talked to me
about menstruation and about the physicalness of
having a baby. She always stressed that it was a very
very hard thing that my birthparents did, giving me
up. She was sure of this although she didn't know who
they were. She told me they must have loved me very
much.

I'm glad my birthparents loved me enough to let me go!

When I was young, I wondered who they might be.
Once I had a dream that my mother was Marilyn
Monroe – but that was only once. I was happy, and I
never had any reason to think about it much.

Once I came across a big stack of sympathy cards
in the garage. I felt awful, terribly jealous, because I
figured Mom and Dad must have had another child. It
took me about two weeks to get up enough nerve to
ask my mom. When I finally asked her, she laughed

and hugged me, and said it was her father who had passed away.

It was about that time I started asking if she had ever been pregnant. She thinks she may have been once, but she fell downstairs, then did some very heavy bleeding.

I have always accepted being adopted and I have always been proud of it. When I was small, I used to run up to people and say, "Hey, I'm adopted!"

People used to ask me who my real parents were. I always said I'm with my real parents. They're all I've ever known. They're super, and I doubt if I could have been happier in any other situation.

It is a hard decision to give up a child – and it takes a lot of love to make that decision. Now that I'm older, I can see how difficult it would be to go through pregnancy, then release for adoption. If you put it in perspective and think about what would be best for the child as far as the future is concerned . . . I'm glad my birthparents loved me enough to let me go!

ADOPTEE SEARCHES FOR BIRTHPARENTS

Some adoptees would like to find their birthparents. Others aren't especially interested. Sometimes an adoptee would like to "search" but is afraid s/he might hurt his/her adoptive parents by doing so. Kellie's adoptive father, however, knew it was important to her to find her birthparents so he helped her search.

Kellie is 19, a college student who grew up in southern California. Her childhood was normal and happy, but by age 10 she decided she wanted to find her other parents. She was eager to tell her story, still excited about her reunion with her birthparents:

I found out I was adopted when I was in kindergarten. Somebody there used the word "adoption" and I didn't know what it meant. I went home and asked Mother and she told me.

She also said I was adopted. I said, "Oh, OK," because when you're five, you don't really care as long as dinner is on the table.

When I was ten it started to bother me. I started having all these feelings about who I was and where I was going. I didn't look like my parents or my sister and I was curious to see if I might look like my birthfamily.

When I was 16 I called a few places but they said I couldn't do anything about finding my birthparents until I was 18. Soon after my 18th birthday my adoptive parents called the adoption agency where they got me. The counselor there gave us some information but she couldn't give me my birthparents' last names.

"Don't I get a hug after all these years?"

I did some detective work on my own – managed to check my hospital birth records and learned my birthmother's name. I was born in a suburb of Los Angeles and had been told she was a college student. I figured if she couldn't afford to keep me, she must have been attending a community college. She probably couldn't afford UCLA or USC.

I went to the library of the city college near her childhood home, asked for the 1966 yearbook. And there it was, my birthmother's picture. I couldn't believe how much she looked like me. Believe me, I was excited!

Then my dad helped me contact a search group. I talked to a woman there and she asked me a lot of

questions. *"What if you find she's dead?"* *"What if
she denies she's your mother?"* *"What if you don't
like her?"* *I told her I wanted to find her and my
birthfather, that I felt I was prepared for whatever
might happen. By then I knew my birthfather's name.*

*She called me a few hours later. She said she had
found my mother's marriage record and had her
current address. She was living only 40 miles away.
I called information and got her phone number.*

*At the time I was seeing a counselor and I asked
him to contact her for me. He called her and said,
"I have someone in my office who has reason to
believe she is your daughter." She was startled to say
the least, and she told the counselor she wanted to talk
with him first.*

He called me the next day and asked me to come over. She was in his office. I said "Hi," and she said, "Don't I get a hug after all these years?" Then she started crying and I said, "Don't do that."

I've seen her nearly every week since then and we talk on the phone. We have a good relationship.

My grandpa kicked her out of the house when she was pregnant and she couldn't afford to keep me. She fed me and spent a lot of time with me while she was in the hospital.

I found my birthfather a couple of months later. I look exactly like him. He had never known my mom was pregnant because he'd gone overseas right after she conceived. His mother, my grandma, was all excited at having another grandchild. She told all their relatives back east, and she can't get over how much we look alike.

"How have your adoptive parents reacted?"

The older I get the more I love my adoptive parents. They've been very caring. They've always given me support, just as they did when I was searching for my birthparents. Of course finding my birthparents hasn't interfered with my relationship with my adoptive parents. But it's wonderful having another set of parents!

PARENTS FIND THEIR BIRTHSON

Lily was 16 when she got pregnant 19 years ago. Her parents sent her to a maternity home with the understanding that adoption was her only option. She released her son a few days after he was born. The whole process was a big secret:

*It was never ever brought up in my house afterward.
My mother never talked about it. Nobody ever said a
word. The first time I ever mentioned it to my mother
was when I told her I was going to search for my son.*

*My baby's father was in the Army and he went to
Germany when I was four months pregnant. By the
time he came back, the baby had been adopted
(father's rights weren't considered then) and I was
back in school. We were married eight months later.*

*When we finally decided to look for Blake, Frank
drove me crazy. He had always wanted to know where
his son was. Once we started, we looked constantly.
We began with the agency. They gave us first names of
our son's adoptive parents and some other information. We had the first names and we had the approxi-
mate date of their marriage so we started checking
marriage records – and we finally found them.*

*We got his adoptive mother's phone number and
called her. When we told her who we were, she started
crying. We discovered she had promised to help Blake
find his birthparents this year. It was something he
had wanted to do for years.*

Blake, a senior in high school, continued the story:

*I'd been duck hunting. When I got home, my older
brother was there and I wondered why. Then my mom
said, "You and Duane come into my room. I want to
talk with you."*

*Whenever she does that, I know I'm going to get it.
"What did I do now?" I asked.*

"Nothing," she replied.

*"Then I've got to go clean my truck," I said. But
she insisted I come in.*

*She told me my birthdad had called, and that he and
my birthmom were married less than a year after I*

was born. They wanted to meet me. My mom seemed happy about it. Of course she had already told me she'd help me look for them.

I've always known I was adopted. It's been fine growing up with my adoptive parents but I used to wonder about my other parents.

I think they (birthparents) did the right thing. If they had kept me, where would we be today? It would have been hard. She was only 16.

Being found has been great. We even videotaped our reunion. I spend most of my weekends with them now and I'm getting acquainted with my three younger brothers. It's really something, having a second family.

SHE'S CURIOUS ABOUT BIRTHMOTHER

Laura was always curious about her birthmother but she was sure her adoptive parents wouldn't want her to search for her. When Carolyn, her birthmother, found her, Laura was surprised and thrilled. She said:

I've always known I was adopted and it seemed a very natural thing. I did envy families who looked alike. I noticed that because my sister (also adopted) and I were totally different, different in the way we looked and different in our personalities. It was special meeting Carolyn and finding that we look so much alike and have a lot in common.

"She knew me right away because we look so much alike."

I was in college when I got the phone call from Carolyn's friend. He told me he had information about my birthmother, that she knew where I was and would like to meet me. He added that Carolyn didn't want to jump into my life if I didn't want that. I learned I had two brothers and a sister. I kind of lost my breath for a second – I couldn't believe this call was coming to me. I had never thought I should look her up. I guess I have a real sense of loyalty to my adoptive parents and I don't want to hurt them.

I told him I'd contact her. That week I wrote Carolyn a long letter and included a photo. The day Carolyn got the letter she called me and we talked for an hour. She lives 500 miles from me, and she flew in to see me a week later.

She knew me right away because we look so much alike. When I saw her I was real tearful and we hugged. People stared at us. We looked so much alike they thought we must be sisters, not mother and daughter.

It's been a lot of fun spending time with Carolyn, but I can't imagine growing up with her. I think it would have been good, but I absolutely would not be who I am today if I had been raised by anyone else. I wouldn't trade my parents in for anyone, not even Carolyn. But I'm very glad I know her.

I was married a year after our reunion and we invited Carolyn and her husband to our wedding. They came, and she's in some of our wedding pictures. She's a very special person. I'm pleased she found me.

Carolyn is proud of her daughter's accomplishments, especially of Laura's graduation from college this spring. Of course she was thrilled to be invited to Laura's wedding. While Carolyn feels some sadness at having missed so much of Laura's life, she knows she had few options 26 years ago. Given those options, she feels she made the right decision. She shared her experiences:

*I was 15 when I became pregnant and my only
option seemed to be adoption. None of the other
options seemed workable so I released her. For twenty
years I assumed I'd never see her again.*

*When I was married four years later, I told my
husband about Laura, but we didn't talk about it. I
never told our kids until after I found her.*

"By this time I had decided — no more secrets."

---

*When Laura was 18 I went back to the agency to
update my records. I said if Laura ever came back and
wanted to meet me, I'd be ready. They had no new
information for me because they had had no contact
with her adoptive family after her placement.*

*A couple of years later I joined an adoption discus-
sion group made up of adoptees and birthparents.
I decided to search for Laura and they helped me.
Within about three months they gave me her name and
a copy of her birth certificate. I discovered which
college her parents had attended and found their
address in the college alumni list. They had moved out
of state three years after Laura was born.*

*If my daughter had been younger, I probably would
have called her parents first, but she was 21. I decided
my friend should call for me. I had to be prepared for
the possibility she wouldn't want to hear from me. Not
all reunions are positive experiences, and I think I was
prepared for whatever might happen.*

*It all turned out as I'd hoped. Laura is a delightful
young woman and my family has enjoyed her visits.*

*After I called her, I knew I had to tell my children
who were 8 and 10. My younger daughter was looking
at family pictures on the wall that day, and she said,
"Mom, if I had a sister, would she look like me?"*

What an opportunity! I said, "As a matter of fact,
you do have a sister." I told her as much as I could
and she was thrilled and excited. She was ready to
dash off to school and tell everybody she had a sister.
By this time I had decided – no more secrets. She told
everybody, and it was OK.

The first letter Laura wrote me was really special.
She included a picture that looked so much like me.
She told me about her interests and I was amazed to
learn how much we were alike.

I called her and we talked for a long time. I said
when she was ready, I'd like to meet her. "What are
you doing tomorrow?" she asked. I flew out to see her
the next week.

It's been a wonderful experience. I'm proud of my
daughter.

MANY ADOPTEES NEVER SEARCH

Do many adult adoptees search for their birthparents? It's
hard to learn how the majority of adoptees feel. The question can be compared to any individual's attitudes toward
learning about his/her family "tree." Some people go to
great lengths to trace their "roots" while others aren't the
least bit interested.

Adoptees' wishes on the matter of searching for birthparents differ too. A father discussed the difference between his two grown children, an adopted son and an
adopted daughter:

My son wanted desperately to find his birthmother.
After much searching, he did find her and was pleased
to learn she was a nice person. She gave him a lot of
family background about his genetic parents and

grandparents. This answered a lot of questions he had had for many years.

He says this has helped him understand why he reacts to certain situations differently than he would expect, considering his life with us. He also says that he feels closer to my wife and me than he ever has, that finding his birthmother actually improved our relationship.

On the other hand, my daughter, also adopted, has shown no interest in finding her birthparents.

Janet expressed feelings much like those of the other adult adoptees I interviewed. I asked her if she had any comments for a 15-year-old whose baby will soon be born, a baby she plans to release for adoption.

She replied:

The love that her adoptive parents will have for your child will be as great as the love you have for him — not necessarily greater, but certainly just as

*great. I really believe that the greatest love a 15- or
16-year-old can have for her baby is to give him up
unless she can get all kinds of support from her family.
A baby gets twice as much love if he has a father to
relate to all the time.*

*From my own experience, I received so much from
my adoptive parents that I am eternally grateful to my
birthmother for the family she gave me.*

12

ADOPTIVE PARENTS' EXPERIENCES

The following item appeared in the Des Moines Register:

I stayed with my parents for several days after the birth of our first child. One afternoon I remarked to my mother that it was surprising our baby had dark hair since both my husband and I are fair. She said, "Well, your daddy has black hair."

"But, Mama, that doesn't matter because I'm adopted."

With an embarrassed smile she said the most wonderful words I've ever heard: "I always forget." (Rodessa E. Morris, Gladys, Va.)

What are adoptive parents like? Are they really "normal" people?

Or perhaps you've read a novel about a poor little orphan

taken in by cold, unloving parents? And she's supposed to
be grateful for everything they've done for her!

You can be sure those cold parents weren't "real." That
story about the poor little orphan is about as fictional as
you can get. Real life adoptive parents are likely to be even
warmer and more loving than some birthfamilies . . .
perhaps because they've waited so long for their children.

"We feel very positive
about Erin's other mother."

With thousands of babies released for adoption each year
in the United States, of course adoptive parents vary a great
deal. Birthparents aren't alike either. Families show lots of
variety. Adoptive families tend to be similar in one characteristic – they love their children very much – just as
nearly all birthparents do. They are also extremely eager to
parent a child.

An adoptive mother commented:

*We moved to California because we'd heard good
things about adoption out here. The first thing we did
was call Children's Home Society. They sent us a form
which invited us to go to a meeting with other people
wanting to adopt a child.*

*It was a room full of people (really only 20), and the
caseworker told us there weren't enough children for
all of us. But if we could stick out the selection
process, she said we might have a child.*

*First we each wrote an autobiography. The case-
worker visited us at home several times and we were
updated quarterly as to what our situation was. We
adopted Erin nine days after she was born. She's been
such a joy to us.*

Sometimes I feel a little guilty about the closeness I

*feel for her because I didn't have quite that much with
our other children. We have two others and I thought I
was close to them. There is a magnetism with Erin that
is really something. She has me wrapped around her
little finger and I love it . . . love it!*

*We have a really positive feeling about Erin's other
mother. She's in college and didn't feel she was ready
yet to be a mother.*

PREGNANCY IMPOSSIBLE FOR MANY COUPLES

One in six couples in the United States today is infertile.
They either cannot conceive or have had a series of miscar-
riages. Many of these couples long for a baby. They keep
appointment after appointment with their doctors, hoping to
"cure" their infertility.

Once a couple accepts the fact that they can't ever have
their own biological child, they may decide they want to
adopt a baby. They may go to a licensed adoption agency,
independent adoption service, or to a doctor or attorney
for help.

---

*"The social worker came out
several times to check us out."*

Often when they adopt a child, they write a letter to their
child's birthparents which reflects the excitement, love and
caring they feel when they finally are able to parent.

Sometimes the adoptive parents meet "their" birthparents, perhaps continue to write to them, send pictures,
possibly see them occasionally after the adoption is finalized. In *Open Adoption: A Caring Option* (Morning Glory
Press), adoptive parents involved in open adoption tell their
stories. They talk about their contacts with the birthparents
of their adopted infants and toddlers.

JOHNSON FAMILY IS DESCRIBED

If you wonder how parents feel about their adopted children during the years they're growing up, consider the Johnsons. They are an example of such a family. Susan and Steve have four children: Eric, 17; Bill, 15; Pat, 13; and Barbara, 10.

Tall and dark-haired Eric is a high achiever at school. He works hard, is rather quiet, and has earned a scholarship to a good university next year.

Stocky Bill is into athletics. He was active in Little League and has won several district awards through his high school swim team activities. He doesn't spend much time on his studies – he's too busy with sports and handling his paper route.

Blond, freckled Pat is also an athlete. She was a Bobby Sox All Star team member this year, is a strong player on her school's basketball team, and is an active participant in track events. She is also active in her church youth group.

Barbara plays the piano well, likes school, but considers athletics to be harder work than she wants. She often offers to help her mother fix dinner, especially if she can make the dessert.

The Johnson children have very different talents, interests, and achievements. Perhaps it's because they're all adopted?

No, that's not the reason – Bill and Eric were adopted, but Pat and Barbara were born to Susan and Steve. Susan shared their story:

We only expected the two boys, and you can imagine how surprised we were when I became pregnant the first time. Then, two years after Pat was born, another miracle – I was pregnant again! We couldn't believe our good fortune . . . a family of four children

*when at one time we thought we might not have any!
If I had it to do over and could choose, I would do
exactly the same thing – adopt Eric and Bill, then give
birth to Pat and Barbara.*

*I really believe these kids are all gifts from God. I
think once you adopt them, they're yours in every
respect, completely, just as if you had them by birth.*

*People have often said that Eric looks exactly like
his dad – he even walks like him. When he was little,
he was a born mimic. It's interesting that Eric looks
more like Steve than either of our birthchildren does.*

*We know Bill's mother had musical talents, and we
have seen it in him almost from the beginning. However, I can't get him to take lessons. He did play the
piano for a few years, but he's too busy with baseball
to think about it now.*

*Several years ago when Bill was in grade school, a
symphony orchestra came to school. They had every
percussion instrument there is and he got so excited.
At that time he was going to be a drummer, and he did
play drums two years in junior high. Now it's all
sports.*

---

*"I've often wondered what
their birthmothers are
thinking on their birthdays."*

---

*When we decided we wanted to adopt a child, we
went to an agency. We were told we had to wait until
we were married five years. Then our doctor asked if
we wanted to adopt independently. We decided to go
ahead. We had been told we couldn't have children by
birth.*

*The social worker from the county came quite a few
times to check us out, sometimes early in the morning.
She was nice but I was always a little nervous. She'd*

sit and talk, and she usually wanted to see the children's rooms. She checked our bank statements occasionally. It took a year for each adoption to become final. Sometimes we'd worry, but mostly we just went along loving the kids.

At first we wondered how to tell them they were adopted. Then someone suggested we mention the word occasionally, and that's what we did. If I saw a friend while I was out shopping, for instance, I'd say, "We just adopted this beautiful baby." We sent out announcements that they were adopted. We never did have to sit down and tell them – they knew and accepted it.

I also told them about their mothers, that each mother had thought it would be better for her son to have another family.

I've often wondered what their birthmothers are thinking on their birthdays. Of course they think of them . . . that's only normal.

I've asked both Eric and Bill if they're interested in finding their birthparents. We have their names and addresses at the time of birth. Bill several years ago asked me what his name would have been and I told him, but he has never mentioned it since. Perhaps they'll want to search later.

Pat sometimes resents the fact that she isn't adopted. I think she said something about it when Eric was critically ill. That's the time you know absolutely they're your own kids whether they're yours by adoption or by birth. You know there is no difference whatsoever.

The Johnsons are unusual in that they had two more children by birth after they had adopted two. A major reason for a couple adopting a child, of course, is because they are infertile (can't get pregnant for some reason). Only about five percent of these couples have a child (or children) by birth after they adopt.

The Johnson's story, unique as it is, is a reassuring answer to that age-old question. "If someone else adopts my baby, would they really treat/love her as their own?"

HOFFMANS CHOOSE OPEN ADOPTION

The Hoffmans have only one child now, but they hope to adopt at least one more. Their daughter, Shontel, is a charming little two-year-old with lovely brown skin and curly hair. She's into everything now, is beginning to talk, and her smile would melt an iceberg.

For 11 years after they were married, Ken and Odette Hoffman tried to have a baby the usual way. Odette would get pregnant as expected, but she was never able to carry a pregnancy to term. She miscarried five heartbreaking times.

When they decided to pursue adoption, they went to a licensed agency which offers as much openness in adoption as is wanted by the birthparents and the adoptive parents. As a result, they see Shontel's mother periodically and are feeling closer and closer to her.

They shared their story:

Odette: *We always knew adoption was an option, but each time we thought, "Well, maybe next time," but each next time was a repeat of the time before. I'd miscarry after two or three months of hoping.*

"We'd been trying to have a baby for eleven years and we realized it wasn't going to happen."

Ken: *Adoption was probably easier for us than for some people. You see, we were both raised in foster families. I lived with my foster family during the week and spent weekends with my first family, my biological parents.*

Odette saw her mother occasionally as she was growing up, but her foster family was her "real" family. This may be why we feel so good about seeing Shontel's mother and being close to her.

Other couples who haven't gone through this thing of belonging to two families might be intimidated. But we know that as Shontel grows up, we can share. We can say, "This is your birthmother," and it's all right.

"When did you decide you wanted to adopt a child?"

Odette: *We'd been trying to have a baby for eleven years and we finally realized it wasn't going to happen. We finally called the agency and got into their orientation program. They did a home study where they talked to me, they talked to Ken, and they talked to us together. You really have to examine how you feel, not just the financial aspect of it, but your heart too. You have to be ready emotionally and be open to meeting the birthmother and going on with an adoption.*

---

*"We were very excited
and we wanted to get
all the information we could."*

When you're thinking about adoption, you have to say, "Well, I know we won't give birth to a child. We really want to go for adoption. This will be our child, not second best, just different from having a biological child.

Ken: *We went to ten hours of classes, two hours per night, where we learned a lot about adoptive parenting. Those classes were a little like a marathon. We started out with lots of couples involved, but some of them didn't stick it out. That was where we started talking about open adoption, and we both decided we wanted as much openness as the birthmother preferred.*

Odette: *We were very excited and wanted to get all the information we could. They gave us this huge packet we had to complete – financial information, marriage license, medical information.You write a lot about yourself and the expectations you have for your baby. For us, this was exciting. Once we had decided to go this route, we rushed through everything. We wanted to get it all done and get our baby.*

Ken: *When we were accepted, when the agency told us we were approved, it was like graduation – except where was our baby? Waiting was a real test for us.*

Odette: *I started keeping a diary the day we first applied, and I still write in it. We saved copies of everything we gave the agency and we'll give it all to Shontel when she's older. I'll show her my diary too.*
We were approved October 16. Every month on the 16th I'd write in my diary. November 16 I wrote, "No baby. What's going on here?" On December 16, "Still no baby. What's happening?" On January 16 all I wrote was a Bible verse focusing on faith.
On January 20, the call came. Karen, our social worker, said, "Guess what – you guys have been chosen to be parents of a little girl." We were terribly excited. We talked until 3 a.m. that first night.

Ken: *We had thought we'd meet the birthmom in*

*her eighth month so we could get prepared. But Karen
said we could pick her up on the 24th. We had three
days to buy the crib, the diapers, the formula, everything. Those were three wild days!*

THEY ARE CHOSEN –
THEY ADOPT SHONTEL

Odette: *After we picked her up, we sat and stared at
her all day. We took pictures like crazy and took them
to the one-hour photo place. The next day we sent
pictures to Monica and to Shontel's birthdad.*

Ken: *We've not met her birthfather, but he sent
Shontel a beautiful letter on Father's Day. He also
sent a little stuffed bear with the letter.*

Odette: *Of course I'm saving the letter and the bear
for her. We didn't meet Monica until Shontel was two
months old. That meeting was at the agency office,
and we didn't exchange last names or addresses then.*

Ken: *That meeting was awkward but friendly. I
have a vivid memory of Monica holding Shontel – we
knew it was important for her to do that – but when
Shontel started to cry, Monica handed her to Odette
and said, "Here, Shontel, go to your mother." When
she said that, I knew Shontel was ours.*

Odette: *We liked Monica right away. The chemistry
was there. We saw her two or three other times that
first year. Then I put our phone number in one of my
letters and she sent us her phone number. Then
Monica called us one day and gave me her address so
I gave her ours. We went out to dinner with her and
her mother a couple of months after that first meeting.*

Ken: *Both Monica and her mother went to
Disneyland with us to celebrate Shontel's first birthday. Our relatives were horrified. "She'll take Shontel
away from you," they warned.*

Odette: *I can't picture the birthparent being bad
because she's the one who wants the best for her
child. We're open to continuing contact with Monica
to whatever degree she wants.*

*When Shontel is older, of course, it will be what she
wants. If there comes a time when she doesn't want to
be with Monica for awhile, we'll continue to exchange
pictures.*

As we were talking, Shontel and her dad were making
faces at each other and carrying on another conversation.
"When Ken's home, I can't do a thing with Shontel. It has
to be her daddy," Odette commented with a smile.

Many adoption agencies do not permit this kind of openness between birth- and adoptive parents. If you think this
is what you'd like, however, discuss it with your adoption
counselor. Even if they haven't done this before, perhaps
they will work with you if you know what you want and are
willing to be a bit assertive about it.

Remember, until you sign the final adoption papers, an
adoption plan for your child is simply that, a plan which, if
it can be worked out to your satisfaction, you'll carry out.
Until you sign the papers, you are the one with the power,
power you can use to plan well for your baby's life.

ONLY CHILD
IS ADOPTED

The Washingtons have only one child. They had hoped to
adopt a second baby but the agency had very few babies
available for placement when they applied. The infants they

did have, the social worker explained, would be placed
with couples who had no children.

---

*"He was the most beautiful
baby we had ever seen.
To our amazement, they let
us take him home right then!"*

Marge and Earl Washington's son, Ralph, is twelve. He
was six weeks old when they adopted him. Marge described their family:

*Our caseworker called one day and said, "We have
a baby, a little boy. Come over and see him and let us
know if you're interested." I was teaching then, and I
had gotten her call after school. I picked Earl up from
work, and we drove over. He was the most beautiful
baby we had ever seen. To our amazement, they let us
take him home right then! We were delighted.*

*I quit my teaching job that same day. We had
applied a year earlier and had been told about ten
months later that we had "passed" the home visits. We
had also been told the wait might be as long as two
years. We don't know why we were called so soon . . .
we never asked!*

*We had a room for him but not much else. Our
neighbors came through with a crib and an infant
seat. Earl made a quick trip to the store for bottles,
formula, and diapers. You can imagine how excited we
were.*

*We had decided to adopt simply because we wanted
a child. We had several friends who had adopted, and
we knew it "worked." We'd been married seven
years, and I just couldn't get pregnant. Doctors told
us I wouldn't be able to have a child of my own – but
we do. Ralph is our own.*

We talked to Ralph about his adoption from the beginning.

In my own family it was no big deal. I had one brother who was a bit skeptical about adoption, but when I put Ralph on his lap, that ended that!

A friend in the throes of morning sickness during her pregnancy once said ruefully that maybe adoption is the easy way to go. I told her that, while I was concerned that she didn't feel well that day, adoption wasn't so easy either. I think if all parents had to go through the soul searching and the questioning that we did with the agency, many might not be parents today.

The Washingtons live in a beautiful home near the mountains. It's a neighborhood deeply involved in Little League, scouting, and PTA activities. According to Marge and Earl, a surprising number of children in their neighborhood are adopted. Marge, who often works as a volunteer aide in Ralph's class at school, reports that at least five children in each grade are adopted:

When we moved here, there were already three families on our block with an adopted child, and we made the fourth. When I learn that a playmate of Ralph's is adopted, I usually throw out a comment to him so if they want to talk about it, they can. Earl says, "You know they don't talk about adoption. All those kids talk about is baseball, 'Star Wars,' whatever, but certainly not adoption!"

We talked to Ralph about his adoption from the beginning. He seldom mentions it, but just yesterday I was measuring him and marking his height on the wall

where we have his "growing chart." I said, "Just
look, Ralph, you weighed only 7 pounds when you
were born, and now you weigh 80."

He said, "Gee, do you suppose my real parents
would be surprised?"

People ask us if we'll be upset if he wants to find his
birthparents when he's grown. We figure that when
he's grown, he'll be his own man. I think he probably
will. Some of his interests are much like his birth-
parents, and some day that may intrigue him.

I've told Ralph more than once that his birthmother
must have had tremendous love for him to be able to
give him up. I personally think that's about the biggest
act of courage possible.

He asked me once why I thought his mother gave
him to us. I told him it wasn't possible for her to care
for him the way she wanted him cared for. She loved
him so much she wanted to give him to someone who
could take care of him as she wanted.

Marge and Earl Washington don't worry about Ralph
contacting his birthmother. They know their love for Ralph
– and his love for them – would not be threatened. In fact,
they compare it to the parents-in-law ties he will probably
have some day. They concluded: "We know we have
enough love for each other – surely we won't be jealous of
his other relationships."

Be assured that adoptive parents can indeed give your
son or daughter as much love and as satisfying a family life
as if s/he were born to them. Witness the Johnson,
Hoffman, and Washington families.

MAKING THE DECISION: WILL I PARENT NOW?

Several years ago the National Alliance for Optional Parenthood developed a questionnaire titled "Am I Parent Material?" It was designed for people not yet pregnant. Purpose was to help them decide whether they wanted a child at this time in their lives.

If you're expecting a baby now, you've already made the decision to become a parent. Your choice is whether to be an active parent to your child or a birthparent who allows someone else to rear her child through adoption.

The following questions are adapted from this questionnaire. Each one deserves careful attention. Answering them may give you additional insight into your feelings about parenting at this time.

Are you keeping a journal during your pregnancy? Writing about your feelings day by day as you progress through this important period in your life might help you with your decision-making. You may want to write in your journal about some of the following questions. There are no "right" answers and no grades. Your answers are right for you and may help you decide for yourself whether or not you want to parent now. If your baby's father is with you, ask him to answer these questions separately, then compare your answers.

You do have a choice. Check out what you know and give it some thought. Then do what seems right for you and for your child.

Does parenting a child now fit the lifestyle I want?

1. What do I want out of life for myself? What do I think is important?

2. Could I handle a child and a job (or school) at the same time? Would I have time and energy for both?

3. Am I ready to give up the freedom to do what I want to do, when I want to do it?

4. Am I willing to cut back my social life and spend more time at home? Will I miss my free time, privacy, and the ability to do what I want when I want?

5. Can I afford to support a child? Do I know how much it costs to raise a child?

6. Do I want to raise a child in the neighborhood where I live now? If not, am I willing and able to move?

7. How would a child interfere with my own growth and development?

8. Would a child change my educational plans?

9. Am I willing to give a great part of my life – at least 18 years – to being responsible for a child? And spend a lot of my life being concerned about my child's well-being?

Do I depend on my parent(s) for support at this time in my life?

1. How would a baby fit into my family's lifestyle?

2. Is there room in our home for another child?

3. Would I have to depend on someone else to take care of my child while I continue school and/or get a job? If so, who would this be?

4. How would I support my child financially this year?

5. How would I support my child during the next 18 years?

6. How do my parents feel about my child living with me/ them?

7. Can my home be child-proofed – that is, can it be arranged so that my child can explore freely when s/he starts to crawl?

8. Am I ready to take on the day-to-day responsibility of parenting – such as handling my child's laundry, cleaning up after him/her, etc., in addition to meeting her/his basic physical and emotional needs?

9. Am I prepared for lots of advice from parents and others if I decide to rear my child myself?

Taking responsibility
for a new life is awesome.

What do I expect from my child?

1. Do I expect my child to make my life happy?

2. Do I want a boy or a girl child? What if I don't get what I want?

3. Will I want my child to be like me?

4. Will I try to pass on to my child my ideas and values? What if my child's ideas and values turn out to be different from mine?

5. Am I expecting a perfect child?

6. Will I want my child to achieve things that I wish I had, but didn't?

7. Will parenting a child show others how mature I am?

Would I enjoy being a parent?

1. Do I like children? When I'm around children, what do I think or feel about having one around all the time?

2. Do I enjoy teaching others?

3. Am I patient enough to deal with the noise and confusion and the 24-hour-a-day responsibility of parenting?

4. What kind of time and space do I need for myself?

5. What do I do when I get angry or upset? Would I take things out on my child if I lost my temper?

6. What does discipline mean to me? What does freedom, or setting limits, or giving space mean? What is being too strict, or not strict enough?

7. How would I take care of my child's health and safety? How do I take care of my own?

8. What if I decide to parent my child and find out I made a wrong decision?

Have my partner and I really talked about becoming parents?

1. Does my partner want to have a child? Have we talked about our reasons?

2. Could we give our child a good home?

3. Is our relationship a happy and strong one?

4. Are we both ready to give our time and energy to raising our child?

5. Can we share our love with a child without jealousy?

6. What would happen if we separated after having our child?

7. Do my partner and I understand each other's feelings about religion, work, family, child raising, future goals? Do we feel pretty much the same way?

8. Will children fit into these feelings, hopes and plans?

These are big questions and many of them are difficult to answer. Please answer them honestly and carefully.

If you decide to parent your child, it will be a decision that will affect you for the rest of your life. Think about it. Taking responsibility for a new life is awesome.

Fermina placed her son with his adoptive family when he was three days old. It was not an easy decision:

> *No matter how many times you say you've made the decision, you haven't until you're in the hospital and you have your child. After the delivery, it all becomes so tangible, so real.*
>
> *I chose to hold my baby, to take care of him those three days. This was important for me to get a grasp on the situation. Every time I touched him there were tears in my eyes. Every time I touched him I made my decision all over again, "I'm going to place him," I'd say. Ten minutes later I'd say, "I'm not going to place him."*
>
> *Before I left the hospital I told him goodbye. The reasons I had decided to place him were still there.*

I couldn't give him the kind of home I wanted for him.

The first letter I got made me sad but it made me feel good too. His adoptive mother told me a lot about him. It made me sad that I couldn't see him, but I was happy they were so pleased and that they appreciated what I did.

I still miss him, of course. It's been four months now, and each week it gets a little easier. I think I made the right decision.

As you know, Fermina's decision was not easy. Neither is yours. One thing is certain – whatever decision you make will be done out of love and caring for your baby. Be proud of that.

APPENDIX

COMPANION VOLUME
FOR *PREGNANT TOO SOON*

The first edition of *Pregnant Too Soon* included longer chapters for parents and for professionals. In this revised edition most of this material is omitted.

First, *Pregnant Too Soon* is meant for young birth-parents, and spending much space on suggestions for their parents and counselors doesn't seem appropriate. In addition, the two chapters provided space only to skim the surface of counseling one's daughter or client facing a too-early pregnancy.

Additional help for parents whose daughter is young and pregnant may be found in *Pregnant Too Soon*'s companion volume, *Parents, Pregnant Teens and the Adoption Option: Help for Families* by Jeanne Warren Lindsay (1988: Morning Glory Press).

Catherine Monserrat, co-author of the widely used *Teenage Pregnancy: A New Beginning,* and Ms. Lindsay are the authors of the forthcoming *Adoption Awareness: A Guide for Counselors, Teachers, Nurses and Caring Others* (1988: Morning Glory Press). This book is designed to help anyone working with young women facing crisis pregnancies.

HELP FOR PARENTS

Pregnant Too Soon is written directly to birthparents. It is they who must make the difficult decisions concerning unplanned pregnancy. It is they who face the loss of their child. It is they who will forever remember this part of their lives.

But teenagers do not exist in limbo. Most pregnant teenagers have parents, parents who have strong opinions about this pregnancy and their grandchild-to-be. Some parents are accepting of the situation, others are appalled. Many are supportive of their daughter (or son) and want to help in any way possible.

NO PERFECT SOLUTION

If your teenage daughter is prematurely pregnant – or if your young son has caused a pregnancy – what is the best solution? What is the "right" thing to do?

Only one thing is certain. There is no perfect solution for too-early pregnancy. Adoption and abortion are both extremely difficult decisions. Neither is single parenting or too-early marriage a good solution for many very young parents.

If she's pregnant, however, she has only these options. She must make a decision – or, if she doesn't, she will simply drift into parenthood. Drifting into parenthood is not a good way to enter that world.

Pregnant Too Soon: Adoption Is an Option encourages decision-making. I do not mean to suggest that every, or even most pregnant teenagers should make adoption plans. I do think, however, that being aware of adoption, then choosing to parent one's child is a much healthier process than is falling into parenthood because there seems to be no other choice.

I have taught a public school program for pregnant teenagers for 15 years. At least a thousand young women have enrolled, and about 40 have released their babies for adoption. Many of the others don't want to hear about adoption. "How could anyone give her baby away?" they ask. Still other students consider adoption, but feel their parents are opposed to such a plan.

For some parents of pregnant teenagers, adoption is unthinkable. This is their grandchild and they are not about to let someone outside the family rear him/her.

Other parents push adoption. They feel parenting at this time would mess up their daughter's (or son's) life. They don't want the responsibility of parenting and they don't think s/he can do it. To them, adoption is the only option.

Parents opposed to adoption need to remember that they probably will not be rearing their grandchild. That task will at some point go to their grandchild's parent(s). Therefore it is extremely important that *they*, not you, make the decision to parent or to release for adoption.

If you are opposed to adoption, try to verbalize your reasons. Is it because you want a grandchild? Are you worried about what your friends and relatives will think? Or is adoption unthinkable "just because"?

You may want to read the experiences of the young women in this book. Each shares her feelings and her decision concerning her unplanned pregnancy. A few explain why they are rearing their children themselves, but the majority are birthmothers who decided adoption would give both themselves and their babies a better chance at satisfying lives.

Hearing these birthmothers share their feelings as they make decisions concerning unexpected pregnancy may help you understand your daughter's feelings a little better.

HELP HER FIND A GOOD COUNSELOR

If your daughter is at all interested in adoption planning, help her find a good counselor. She is most likely to receive counseling concerning her options if she goes to a licensed adoption agency.

You can assure her that talking with an adoption counselor does not imply she has already decided to release her baby for adoption. Several counselors from adoption agencies have told me that less than half of their clients actually release their babies for adoption. The agency's purpose is to help young women make their own decisions about unplanned pregnancy, *not* to make those decisions for them.

If the adoption is planned through a lawyer or doctor, the risk is great that the birthparents will receive no counseling. Delivering a child, then releasing that child to someone else to parent is a real crisis. Young birthparents need help in dealing with this crisis.

In some areas, independent adoption centers provide counseling services similar to those offered by licensed adoption agencies. One risk in independent adoption is the possibility of the money involved in an adoption, which is paid by the adoptive parents, becoming more important than is meeting the needs of the birthparents.

As far as independent adoption is concerned, my bias is slightly toward church-affiliated independent adoption services. Within these groups there may be a better chance of the needs of the birthparent taking precedence over the income generated by providing babies for adoptive parents.

Your daughter might appreciate help in connecting with either an agency or independent adoption service. Perhaps you can provide that help.

IF SHE CHOOSES TO PARENT NOW

If your daughter decides to keep her baby to rear herself, you can help her deal with some of the practical aspects of early parenting. Where will she live? How will she support her child? Will she continue to live with you while she completes school? Who will take primary responsibility for the baby?

The questions could go on and on. You will need to have many conversations dealing with these questions *before* the baby is born. It is always better to be prepared for crises before they happen. A new baby in the house, sweet as s/he may be, is definitely a crisis, especially if that baby's parent is very young and single.

If the decision is to parent, it is important that she/they do a good job of parenting. *Teens Parenting: The Challenge of Babies and Toddlers* is a good parenting guide for very young parents. (See Bibliography.) Teenage mothers share their experiences in parenting their babies and toddlers. A great deal of solid parenting information is incorporated into the text.

If the young couple is considering marriage, *Teenage Marriage: Coping with Reality* offers guidance. If they (or

you) want to learn more about teenagers' attitudes toward
and expectations for marriage, they (and you) will find
Teens Look at Marriage: Rainbows, Roles and Reality
helpful. Both marriage books are based on extensive interviews with young couples already married or living together as teenagers and on a nationwide survey of more
than 3000 teenagers' attitudes toward marriage. *Teens Look
at Marriage* is an account of this research.

Whatever decision your daughter (or son) makes about
an unplanned pregnancy, s/he needs your love and your
support. You can help her/him understand the responsibilities involved in parenting, and you can help her/him look at
options. The final decision, however, will not be yours.

Additional and more detailed information and suggestions for parents of pregnant teenagers are included in
Pregnant Too Soon's companion book, *Parents, Pregnant
Teens and the Adoption Option: Help for Families.* Parents
of teenagers share their experiences as they help their
daughters cope with too-early and unexpected pregnancy.

Also included in this book are excerpts from the journal
a midwestern couple kept during their daughter's unplanned pregnancy. Their concern as they talk about their
daughter and her adoption decision may mirror yours.

Your love and concern for your daughter (or son) is
especially important now. Whether s/he makes an adoption
plan or decides to rear the baby, your caring and your
support are crucial.

The parents who truly support their daughter as she
makes her own decision may merit the high praise
bestowed on her mother by Jodie:

> *I feel parents are a very important part of this. I
> didn't find out until I was pregnant that my mother is
> the best friend I have. A girl really needs her mother –
> and her father – at that point. My mom went through
> as much as I did, maybe more, because I was her*

daughter and this was her grandson.

*I think it's because of my mother that I'm where I
am today. My decision to release my baby for adoption was right for me – but I needed my mother's
support and I got it.*

The support of her parents can be very important to a
young woman with an unplanned pregnancy. Many young
people have told me this has been a time of drawing closer
to their parents. It may be a difficult time for everyone, but
together, they may find the decision most "right" for everyone involved.

WORKING WITH
BIRTHPARENTS

If you work with pregnant teenagers, do you attempt to create a climate for adoption as well as parenting? Some people working with women with unplanned pregnancies seldom if ever mention adoption. They know adoption is not a popular decision. Perhaps they assume it is an impossible decision. Or they may feel that mentioning such an unpopular subject might   alienate their clients.

Each of these reasons may be valid at times. But by simply assuming that our clients are opposed to adoption, we may really be saying, "I know what's best for you and you can't/shouldn't consider adoption."

Just as we have no right to be judgmental of our clients, we have no right to decide who should and who shouldn't consider an adoption plan. We have no right to push a client toward either adoption or keeping. We do have a right and a responsibility to help each client and her family understand her options.

Most teenagers know little or nothing about adoption. Few adults know the agencies available in their area, the pros and cons of agency versus independent adoption.

Our first task as helping persons is to become as knowledgeable as possible about adoption resources in our area. We also need to be well-informed about legal requirements concerning adoption in our state or province.

Collecting a resource list can be done by telephone although in-person information gathering often works best. Talk to several adoption agency and independent adoption service counselors in your community. If there is a lawyer who specializes in adoption, contact him/her.

After you have completed your survey, create a handout for your clients. A flyer containing this information can help a young woman become informed.

Briefly explain the legal requirements for adoption. List resources for agency and independent adoption in your community. (A few states do not allow an independent adoption plan.)

Describe the services available from each, and include the name and phone number of a contact person for each. Determine the degree of openness allowed/advocated by each resource and share this information with your client.

Phyllis, unhappy mother of a two-year-old, has some suggestions for people working with pregnant teenagers:

> *You could explain to a person that you do have an option. It wouldn't work to say, "I think you should put your baby up for adoption because you're not ready for it," but you could point out how it will be with a child – there are too many responsibilities, so many things to take care of, especially when you don't have a father to help. When you're so young, you just don't realize what you're getting into. And you can't depend on welfare to support you all your life. You can't do that because you're not going to get anywhere on welfare.*
>
> *I think more people should talk to the girls about adoption. Get someone to come in and tell the girls*

about the bad parts of being a parent. Get somebody
to talk to them. Tell them it's tough to be a mother,
especially if you're trying to raise a kid by yourself.

Find out what your client knows about adoption. If she is
completely opposed to discussing the subject, you'll respect
her thinking, but you'll know she is aware of her adoption
option. Your next step may be to help her prepare for her
future parenting role.

ENCOURAGE PEERS TO BE SUPPORTIVE

If you work with a group of pregnant teenagers, you will
want each to accept totally the decisions the others make.
You don't want someone saying to a young woman considering an adoption plan, "How could you possibly give your
baby away?" Neither do you want anyone putting somebody down, perhaps a 14-year-old planning to rear her
child herself, by saying, "You can't possibly raise a baby
yourself."

I find the former statement is likely to be heard from
teenagers, and the latter from older people. Neither shows
respect for the individual involved.

Those opposed to adoption may know very little about
the subject. To them, making an adoption plan means the
birthmother doesn't care about her baby. Helping them
understand the love and unselfishness involved in releasing
one's child to another family may enable them to be supportive of peers considering such a plan.

SPECIAL CLASS FOCUSES ON ADOPTION

In my prenatal health class I offer a brief unit on adoption every couple of months. I explain the changes

occurring in adoption today. I emphasize the fact that open adoption is available if desired I stress that birthparents who release do so out of love and concern for their babies. It is not a selfish decision. In fact, it often is the most *unselfish* decision possible.Birthparents, adoptive parents, adoptees, and adoption counselors are invited to speak to the class. Reading assignments deal with the adoption option.

Never do I mean to imply that everyone, or any specific individual *should* make an adoption plan. Instead I stress the importance of choosing to parent rather than feeling trapped into parenting. I also emphasize that each of us needs to know something about adoption – at least the legal aspects and the various alternatives available – so that we can be knowledgeable about an important topic.

PROVIDING HELP FOR BIRTHGRANDPARENTS

When we work with pregnant teenagers, we need always to remember that many of our clients are living with and deeply influenced by their families. Sometimes a young woman makes an adoption plan, appears to be firm in her decision, only to change her mind in the hospital because her parents suddenly decide they want their grandchild.

The young woman may understand the grieving process and know there's nothing easy about adoption. If she has worked through these things, she may be able to handle the adoption decision far better than her parents can.

For more understanding of the role of birthgrandparents in adoption planning, see *Parents, Pregnant Teens and the Adoption Option: Help for Families.* (1988: Morning Glory Press) by Lindsay.

For an extremely helpful and detailed discussion of pregnancy counseling in general, see *Adoption Awareness: A Guide for Counselors, Teachers, Nurses and Caring Others* by Catherine Monserrat and Jeanne Warren Lindsay (1988: Morning Glory Press).

ANNOTATED BIBLIOGRAPHY

FOR BIRTHPARENTS

The following books for birthparents deal primarily with the dilemma of unplanned pregnancy. Some focus on decision-making generally, others on adoption specifically. Others provide guidance during pregnancy, while some stress the realities of parenting a child and/or premature marriage.

Prices, when given, are from the 1987 edition of *Books in Print*. If you order a book directly from the publisher, check first with your public library or a bookstore to learn current prices. Then add $2.00 for shipping.

Barr, Linda, and Catherine Monserrat. *Teenage Pregnancy: A New Beginning*. Revised 1987. New Futures, Inc., 2120 Louisiana NE, Albuquerque, NM 87110. Also available from Morning Glory Press, 6595 San Haroldo Way, Buena Park, CA 90620. 98 pages. Illustrated. $10. Quantity discount. Spanish edition also available: Un Nuevo Comienzo.

This book was written specifically for pregnant adolescents. Topics include prenatal health care, nutrition during pregnancy, fetal development, preparation for labor and delivery, decision-making, emotional effects of adolescent pregnancy, and others. The authors have obviously known, worked with, and loved many school-age parents.

Anderson, Carole, Lee Campbell, and Mary Anne Manning Cohen. *Choices, Chances, Changes: A Guide to Making an Informed Choice About Your Untimely Pregnancy.* 1981: CUB, Inc., P.O. Box 573, Milford, MA 01757. 63 pages. $5.00.

Book offers constructive suggestions for questions a young person should ask if she approaches an adoption agency for help. Mainly it is a reassuring booklet for young mothers who want to keep their babies to rear themselves.

Arms, Suzanne. *To Love and Let Go.* 1983: Alfred A. Knopf, New York. Hardcover, 228 pages. $14.95.

Presents the stories of several young women who release their babies for adoption and of the parents these birthmothers choose. Arms' emphasis is on the needs of the birthmothers and of the positive effects of adoptive parents and birthparents meeting and developing a relationship.

Becker, Kayla M., with Connie K. Heckert. *To Keera with Love.* 1987. Sheed and Ward, Kansas City. Paper, $7.95. Also available from Morning Glory Press, 6595 San Haroldo Way, Buena Park, CA 90620.

Dramatic true story of Kayla's journey from a protected, happy childhood to the harsh reality of becoming a mother too soon, and through her grieving as she places her beloved Keera for adoption.

Ewy, Donna and Rodger. *Teen Pregnancy: The Challenges We Faced, The Choices We Made.* 1985. Pruett Publishing Company, Boulder, CO. $14.95. New American Library. Paper, $3.95.

A refreshingly practical guide for teenagers facing the hard choices and special challenges of pregnancy in the teen years. Good advice is coupled with many quotes from pregnant and parenting teenagers.

Hansen, Caryl. *Your Choice: A Young Woman's Guide to Making Decisions About Unmarried Pregnancy.* 1980. Paper. Avon. $2.25.

A comprehensive guide to the options open to pregnant teenagers.

The author emphasizes the need for choosing an option rather than going into motherhood without making a decision. Suggested is a "Pregnancy Timeline" to be used in decision-making.

Johnson, Joy and Dr. S. M., Mary Vondra and Martha Jo Church. *Pregnant – This Time It's Me. 1985*. 24 pp. Centering Corporation, Box 3367, Omaha, NE 68103-0367. $2.45.

Feelings – feeling scared, feeling angry, feeling sorry for oneself, feeling guilty, and feeling alone – and dealing with these feelings are stressed throughout this booklet.

Johnston, Patricia Irwin, Ed. *Perspectives on a Grafted Tree. 1983*: Perspectives Press, Hardcover. 144 pages. $12.95.

A beautiful collection of poems written by birthparents, adoptees, adoptive parents, and extended family members. They express a wide variety of both positive and negative feelings which are part of the gains and losses, happiness and pain felt by all those touched by adoption.

Lindsay, Jeanne Warren. *Do I Have a Daddy? A Story About a Single-Parent Child.* Illustrated by DeeDee Upton Warr. 1982. 46 pp. Color. Morning Glory Press, 6595 San Haroldo Way, Buena Park, CA 90620. Hardcover, $7.95. Paper, $3.95.

This is a picture book/story in which a single mother explains to her son that his daddy left soon after he was born. It contains a 12-page section of suggestions for single parents.

_____. *Open Adoption: A Caring Option.* 1987. 256 pp. Photos. Morning Glory Press. Hardcover, $15.95; paper, $9.95.

A fascinating and sensitive account of the new world of adoption where birthparents choose their child's adoptive parents and may remain in contact with their child's new family. Written for birthparents, adoptive parents, and professionals.

_____. *Teenage Marriage: Coping with Reality. 1988*. 108 pp. Photos. Morning Glory Press. Hardcover, $15.95. Paper, $9.95. Teacher's guide, $5.95. Student study guide, $2.50.

Marriage book written especially for teenagers. Based on in-depth interviews with married teens and on nationwide survey of teenagers' attitudes toward marriage. Extremely realistic.

_____. *Teens Parenting: The Challenge of Babies and Toddlers*.
1981. 308 pp. Illustrated by Pam Patterson Morford. Morning Glory
Press. Hardcover, $14.95; paper, $9.95. TG, $5.95. SG, $2.50.

Basic how-to-parent book based on interviews with 61 teenage
mothers. Their comments are incorporated throughout the book.
Sixth grade reading level.

McGuire, Paula. *It Won't Happen to Me: Teenagers Talk About
Pregnancy*. 1983. Delacourte, 234 pp. $14.95. Dell, 1986, $7.95.

Fifteen teenagers talk about their unplanned pregnancies, the
decisions they made, and the changes in their lives.

Myers, Walter Dean. *Sweet Illusions*. 1986. Teachers & Writers
Collaborative. 142 pp. Hardcover, $9.95; paper, $3.95. Available
from Morning Glory Press, Inc.

Absorbing fictional accounts of lives of very young mothers and
fathers. Wonderful reading/writing curriculum for English classes.

O'Brien, Bev. *Mom, I'm Pregnant*. 1982. Tyndale. 125 pp. $4.95.

Written by the mother of a pregnant teenager, this book has a strong
religious slant. Emphasis is on the adoption decision.

Pierson, Anne. "My Baby and Me: Basic Decision-Making." 1984.
Loving & Caring, Inc., 100 Foxshire Drive, Lancaster, PA 17601
34-page workbook. $3.00.

Packed with "thinking" questions concerning goals in life, plans for
the baby, and other areas of concern for pregnant teenagers.

Richards, Arlene Kramer, and Irene Willis. *What to Do If You or
Someone You Know Is Under 18 and Pregnant*. 1983. 254 pp.
Lothrop, $10.88. Paper, $7.00.

A very readable discussion of possible alternatives.

Roggow, Linda, and Carolyn Owens. *A Handbook for Pregnant
Teenagers*. Zondervan, Paper, $5.95.

Appropriate for young women whose religious convictions make abortion an impossible choice. Alternatives of marriage, adoption, and raising the baby alone are presented.

Roles, Patricia. *Facing Teenage Pregnancy: A Handbook for the Pregnant Teen.* 1984. Eterna Press, P.O. Box 1344, Oak Brook, IL 60521. 123 pp. Paper, $5.95.

This is a personal guidebook with a non-directive and supportive approach. Included are several first-person accounts of early pregnancy, adoption, abortion, and parenthood.

Silber, Kathleen, and Phylis Speedlin. *Dear Birthmother: Thank You for Our Baby.* 1983. 193 pp. Corona Publishing Company, 1037 S. Alamo, San Antonio, TX 78210. Trade, $7.95.

An excellent book. Refutes such myths of adoption as the idea that birthparents don't care about their babies. Includes many beautiful letters from adoptive parents to birthparents and from birthparents to adoptive parents.

Witt, Reni L., and Jeannine Masterson Michael. *Mom, I'm Pregnant! A Personal Guide for Teenagers.* 1982. Stein & Day. 239 pp. $6.95.

Excellent book for young people facing decisions about unplanned pregnancy.

BOOKS FOR PARENTS/PROFESSIONALS

Most of the following titles deal with the needs of birthparents. Many other books are available which focus on adoptive parents and/or adoptees.

Barr, Linda, and Catherine Monserrat. *Working with Childbearing Adolescents: A Guide for Use with Teenage Pregnancy, A New Beginning.* New Futures Inc. Also available from Morning Glory Press. Revised 1986. Spiral, $12.95.

Introductory chapter presents overview of teen pregnancy and parenthood in the United States. In addition, adolescent development and sexuality are explored. Authors include their experiences, ideas, and insights gained through working with pregnant adolescents.

Brandsen, Cheryl Kreykes, M.S.W. A *Case for Adoption: A Guide to Presenting the Option of Adoption*. 1985. Bethany Christian Services, 901 Eastern N.E., Grand Rapids, MI 49503. 48 pp. $2.00.

Well-written booklet designed for counselors who work with pregnant teenagers. It stresses respect and caring concern for birthparents, and does not suggest that adoption is the only option a young person could or should choose. Rather, it addresses the concerns and frustrations counselors have expressed about representing adoption as a loving, responsible, and mature choice that must be considered as seriously as parenting or marriage.

Lindsay, Jeanne Warren. *Parents, Pregnant Teens and the Adoption Option: Help for Families*. 1988. Morning Glory Press. Hardcover, $12.95; Paper, $7.95.

Guidance for parents of pregnant teenagers. Offers practical suggestions for providing support while encouraging the young person to take responsibility for her decisions. Includes experiences of and suggestions from parents and counselors.

_____. *Teens Look at Marriage: Rainbows, Roles and Reality*. 1985. 256 pp. Photos. Morning Glory Press. Hardcover, $15.95. Paper, $9.95. Study Guide, $2.50.

An in-depth coverage of the research behind *Teenage Marriage: Coping with Reality*. Attitudes of teenagers not yet married are compared with those who are. Provides insight into world of teenage couples. 34 bar graphs, 130 tables, 8 photos.

Meezan, William, and Sanford Katz. *Adoptions Without Agencies: A Study of Independent Adoptions*. 1977. New York: Child Welfare League of America. Paper, $13.50.

A report of research of independent adoption as experienced by birthparents and adoptive parents. Legal and psychological risks of independent adoption are outlined, but authors do not recommend outlawing all independent adoption. Rather, they suggest a number of changes in agency and independent adoption practices, changes which could make adoption more satisfying to all those involved.

Monserrat, Catherine, and Jeanne Warren Lindsay. *Adoption Awareness: A Guide for Counselors, Teachers, Nurses and Caring Others.* 1988. Morning Glory Press, Inc. Hardcover, $15.95. Paper, $9.95.

Wonderful book for teachers, counselors, social workers, nurses, and others working with pregnant teenagers and/or older women facing untimely pregnancy. Offers an in-depth look at current adoption issues including agency, independent, and open adoption. Emphasis is on the needs of the birthparents.

Mueller, Candace P. *The Adoption Option: A Guidebook for Pregnancy Counselors.* 1986. 72 pages. Project SHARE, P.O. Box 2309, Rockville, MD 20852.

This guidebook was developed and written under the auspices of the Office of Population Affairs of the Department of Health and Human Services. It provides a general explanation of the adoption process and highlights important points that counselors should be aware of in counseling young women about adoption.

Pierson, Anne. *Mending Hearts, Mending Lives.* 1987. Loving & Caring, Inc. 156 pages. $4.95.

Book written for families providing shelter in their homes for single pregnant women. Offers excellent guidance and shows real respect and caring for the young women involved.

Rillera, Mary Jo, and Sharon Kaplan. *Cooperative Adoption: A Handbook.* 1984: Triadoption Publications, P.O. Box 638, Westminster, CA 92684. 158 pages. Paper. $14.95.

Offers excellent guidelines for birthparents and adoptive parents
· planning an open adoption. Authors do not recommend co-parenting except in the sense of both sets of parents being actively involved with the child. The adoptive parents are the legal and psychological day-to-day parents, but the birthparents may be as close to the adoptive family as desired by everyone involved. Suggested cooperative adoption documents are included.

ABOUT THE AUTHOR

Jeanne Warren Lindsay, M.A., developed and now coordinates the Teen Mother Program, an alternative offered to pregnant and parenting students in the ABC Unified School District, Cerritos, California. This program is a choice offered to pregnant and parenting students who do not wish to attend the comprehensive high school throughout pregnancy. Ms. Lindsay has counseled hundreds of pregnant teenagers in her 15 years in this position.

Ms. Lindsay has advanced degrees in home economics and anthropology. She is a member of the Board of Directors of the National Organization on Adolescent Pregnancy and Parenthood, and editor of the *NOAPP Network*. She frequently gives presentations on adoption, the culture of school-age parents, teenage marriage, educating pregnant and parenting teens, and other topics.

She is the author of six other books concerned with adoption, adolescent pregnancy and parenthood, and teenage marriage.

She and Bob have been married for 36 years. They have five grown children.

INDEX

Adoptees, adult, 167-180

Adoption counseling, 45, 55-57, 59, 75, 156-157, 205-206, 209-212

Adoption expense, 81, 92-93

Adoption information resources, 53

Adoption law, 49, 69-72, 111, 115-118, 131, 133, 210

Adoption petition, 85

Adoptions without Agencies: A Study of Independent Adoptions, 94

Adoptive parents, 36, 59-62, 64-65, 81, 85, 87, 91-93, 96, 110-112, 140-145, 148, 149-150, 157, 165, 181-194

Adoptive parents, preparation of, 60-62, 80, 85, 182, 188-189

Agency adoption, 24, 53-82, 83-98, 205, 210

Alleged father, 118-119, 120-121

"Am I ready to be a parent" questionnaire, 51-52, 195-200

American Indian adoption, 112

Anemia, 27

Birth certificate, 70-71

Birthfather, 64, 72-74, 76, 79, 101-102, 107, 111, 115-124, 133-135, 138, 145-146, 147, 158-159, 161-164, 196, 198-199

Birthgrandparents, 197, 203-208, 212

Black adoption, 60, 112-113

California law, 116-119

Children's Defense Fund, 28

Children's Home Society, 55-60, 78, 154, 156

Consent to adoption, 84

Counseling resources, 53, 205-206

De Armond, Charlotte, 121

Dear Abby, 106

Decision-making, 48-50

Divorce, 29, 30-32

Edson, James, 97-98

Education, 31-32, 37, 40, 43, 47-48, 56, 63-64

Financial assistance, 81

Financial responsibility, 37

Foster care, 81-82, 131

Garrison, Tanelle, 151-152

Gibran, Kahlil, 135-136

Gomell, Julie, 26-28

Grandparents, 33

Grief, 65, 88, 103, 105, 125-136, 164

Hispanic adoption, 60, 112-113

Hospital personnel, 67, 80, 88

Independent adoption, 24, 53, 83-98, 205-206, 210

Independent adoption services, 84, 95-97

Infertility, 183, 186-187, 192

Information requirement act, 71

La Leche League, 58-59

Lawyer, 84, 87, 89-92, 94, 95, 97-98

Leavitt, David, 90-92, 98

Letters, 57, 133, 137-150, 157

Marriage, 15, 29-32, 74

Minority adoption, 60, 112-113

Miscarriage, 24

Monserrat, Catherine, 11-14

Moses, 117

Myers-Rick, Jennifer, 21

Native American adoption, 112

Open adoption, 16, 36, 54-55, 83, 87,95-97, 114, 129, 183, 187-191

Open Adoption: The Caring Option, 215, 55, 183

Parents, Pregnant Teens and the Adoption Option: Help for Families, 202, 207, 212

Parents' reaction to daughter's pregnancy, 40, 45, 62-63, 66, 74, 85, 95, 101, 121-122, 161

Peer influence, 57, 66, 86, 104, 211-212

Post-adoption counseling, 72

Poverty, 28

Premature birth, 27

Presumed father, 118-119, 120-121

Relative adoption, 24, 99-114

Release form, 69

Repeat pregnancy, 79

Richardson, Julia, 60

School program for pregnant teens, 16, 40, 63, 66, 76-75, 86, 102, 204

School-age parenthood, 26-28, 42-48, 50-51, 107-110, 206

Schwiebert, Patricia, 127

Sealed records, 70, 71, 171

Searching, adoptees, 68, 88-89, 133, 173-175, 194

Searching, birthparents, 68, 88-89, 133, 173-175-178, 181-194

Secrecy in adoption, 24, 54, 70-71, 126, 137, 167-168, 170

Seeing baby, 42, 129, 131-132

Stebbins, Jennifer, 54, 129, 133

Teenage marriage, 15, 29-32, 45, 74

Teenage Marriage: Coping with Reality, 206

Teens Look at Marriage, 207

Teens Parenting: The Challenge of Babies and Toddlers, 206

Toddler adoption, 132, 151-166, 178

Toxemia, 27

Two-parent family, 37

Uniform Adoption Act, 70, 116, 118

Wills, Janice, 60, 71, 120-121, 129

MORNING GLORY PRESS
6595 San Haroldo Way, Buena Park, CA 90620
714/828-1998

Specializing in books focusing
on adolescent pregnancy and parenthood, adoption,
and teenage marriage Write for current catalog.

Please send me the following:

Quantity	Title	Price	Total

PREGNANT TOO SOON: ADOPTION IS AN OPTION

____	Paper, ISBN 0-930934-25-3	$9.95	_____
____	Cloth, ISBN 0-930934-26-1	15.95	_____

PARENTS, PREGNANT TEENS AND THE ADOPTION OPTION

____	Paper, ISBN 0-930934-27-X	7.95	_____
____	Cloth, ISBN 0-930934-28-4	12.95	_____

OPEN ADOPTION: THE CARING OPTION

____	Paper, ISBN 0-930934-23-7	9.95	_____
____	Cloth, ISBN 0-930934-22-9	15.95	_____

TEENAGE PREGNANCY: A NEW BEGINNING

____	Spiral	10.00	_____

WORKING WITH CHILDBEARING ADOLESCENTS

____	Spiral	12.95	_____

TEENS PARENTING: THE CHALLENGE OF BABIES AND TODDLERS

____	Paper, ISBN 0-930934-11-3	9.95	_____
____	Cloth, ISBN 0-930934-07-5	14.95	_____

TEENAGE MARRIAGE: COPING WITH REALITY

____	Paper, ISBN 0-930934-11-3	9.95	_____
____	Cloth, ISBN 0-930934-12-1	15.95	_____

TEENS LOOK AT MARRIAGE: RAINBOWS, ROLES AND REALITY

____	Paper, ISBN 0-930934-15-6	9.95	_____
____	Cloth, ISBN 0-930934-16-4	15.95	_____

DO I HAVE A DADDY? A STORY ABOUT A SINGLE-PARENT CHILD

____	Paper, ISBN 0-930934-17-2	3.95	_____
____	Cloth, ISBN 0-930934-10-5	7.95	_____

QUANTITY DISCOUNTS   **TOTAL** _____

Please add postage: 1-3 books, $1.50; 4+, .50 per book   _____

California residents - add 6% sales tax   _____

TOTAL ENCLOSED   _____

Prepayment requested. School/library purchase orders accepted.

If not satisfied, return in 15 days for refund.

Quantity discount.

NAME _____

ADDRESS _____